The Techniques

Indian Embroidery

The Techniques of

Indian Embroidery

Anne Morrell

INTERWEAVE PRESS

To Grace and Sam Isaac

Acknowledgements

My thanks to Chris Eden of Seattle, Francis French, Trevor Jones and Terry Waddington, who kindly photographed the work illustrated in this book.

My thanks also to all the people who helped me and loaned me work, in particular Alexander Walker, Judy Sourakli, Penny Oakely, Anthea Jarvis, Dr S.D. Trevedi, D.S. Mehta, Mr Desai, Meira Stockl, Mr and Mrs Chandran, Dr and Mrs Chan Sandhu, John Gillow, Joss Graham, Karen Burns, Sylvia Wood and Thelma Nye.

Anne Morrell
Manchester 1992

Slide packs on Indian embroidery by Anne Morrell are available. Further information can be obtained from:

The Slide Librarian
Manchester Metropolitan University
Righton Building
Cavendish Street
Manchester MI5 6BG

Copyright 1995, Anne Morrell

Typeset by Express Typesetting Limited
Printed in Hong Kong by Sing Cheong

 Interweave Press, Inc.
201 East Fourth Street
Loveland, Colorado 80537
USA

Library of Congress Cataloging-in-Publication Data
CIP applied for.

ISBN 1-883010-08-X

First printing:IWP—7.5M195:CC

FRONT JACKET:
Woman's skirt fragment, 90 x 81 cm (35½ x 32 in). Gujarat, Kutch, nineteenth century. Plain-weave, satin-weave and embroidered (ACC. NO. 58.2-116, ELIZABETH BAYLEY WILLIS COLLECTION, HENRY ART GALLERY, UNIVERSITY OF WASHINGTON)

BACK JACKET:
Rumal. *Plain-weave, embroidered, painted and block-printed by hand, 55·9 x 55·6 cm (22 x 21¾ in). Himachal Pradesh, Chamba, India. Nineteenth century* (ACC. NO. 58.2-107, ELIZABETH BAYLEY WILLIS COLLECTION, HENRY ART GALLERY, UNIVERSITY OF WASHINGTON)

PAGE 2:
Detail of a phulkari. *Punjab, early twentieth century*

PAGE 3:
Embroidery to go over a door, embellished with tin-framed mirrors, 107 x 51 cm (42 x 20 in). Gujarat, 1970s

Contents

Historical background

BC	**30,000**			Stone Age settlers in India
			3500	Expansion of agricultural settlements, Indus area
			2500	Mohenjo-daro flourishing, declined *c.* 1750
	1500–1000			Indo-Aryans enter India, particularly the Punjab
		1368–1349		Tutankhamun's reign (Egyptian New Kingdom 1567–1085)
	1000–600			Indo-Aryan migration, Ganges valley settled
	600–326	**563–480**		The Buddha living and preaching
			530	Persians invade Indus valley
			326	Alexander the Great crosses Indus into Punjab
	326–185			Mauryan Empire
			221	Building of the Great Wall of China (existing wall mainly restored in the period 1368–1644 AD)
	185 BC –	AD **300**		Nomad invasions
		AD **73**		Fall of Masada (by the Dead Sea)
AD	**320–495**			Gupta Empire
				Ajanta paintings
	711–1193			Islam comes to India
			711	Arabs invade the Sind
		1001–1030		Mahmud of Ganga plunders the Punjab and Gujarat
	1193–1526			Domination of Turco-Afghan forces
			1193	Turco-Afghan forces conquer Delhi
	1526–1756			Moghal Empire
			1632	Work starts on the Taj Mahal
			1612	English merchants start trade in Surat (south of Bombay)
			1642	English establish East India Company in Madras
			1698	English establish East India Company in Calcutta
	1707–1756			Disintegration of the Moghal Empire
	1756–1858			Rise of the British Empire
			1853	First cotton mill starts in Bombay

1858–1947		British Imperialism
	1885	Indian National Congress founded
	1911	Capital transferred from Calcutta to New Delhi
	1947	Independence
1947–present day	**1947**	Formation of Pakistan
	1971	Formation of Bangladesh, formerly East Pakistan

Introduction

Embroidery is the embellishment of fabric, enriching it with a needle and thread. Gaining an understanding of the overall historical development of embroidery is not an easy task, but understanding the origins perhaps makes it easier to see why there are many and varied techniques which come under the general heading of 'embroidery'. Some embroidery stitches undoubtedly have their foundation in early textiles, basketry, mat-making and weaving; others have developed from early sewing, where stitches were used for joining pieces of fabric or skins together for specific ornamental purposes.

In gaining an understanding of Indian embroidery it is important to consider India's position in relation to other countries, and its past trade, invasions and migration patterns. As a result of these factors, changes have been considerable, not least during the twentieth century. In the early part of the century, any study of India would have involved the whole subcontinent, but this area has now been divided into the countries of Pakistan, Bangladesh and India. The

natural movement of peoples throughout the subcontinent means that similar embroidery can be found throughout these countries, despite the formation of national boundaries. There are only a few techniques which have become localized in an area outside that now known as India. One of these is a form of *phulkari* embroidery (see pages 55–67) which is produced in Swat, in Pakistan.

India lies along the ancient trade routes across Asia. This has resulted in the introduction of many cultural and religious influences from other countries. From the West came trade and influence, from Iran (Persia), from the Aegean area, and from Afghanistan. From the East, notably along the old silk roads, came the rich textiles from China. India has a very extensive coastline, and for centuries this has enabled trade to flourish with many countries, including Portugal, Holland, France and Britain. These became invaders rather than trading partners, with obvious effects on the cultures and crafts of India. The areas around Bengal and Gujarat have, for hundreds of years, been notable centres for European trading companies, exporting large quantities of embroideries and other textiles.

Probably the major influence on Indian textiles was the Persian taste and tradition which prevailed during the Moghal Empire (1526-1756). Other significant influences came from the Europeans, including the British. India has assimilated and made its own many of the ideas introduced by these people and, throughout history, has been renowned for the diversity, quality and richness of its textiles. Study of the arts and crafts of ancient times is usually confined to evidence gained from the remains of hard objects, such as stone carvings or ceramic pieces, and examples of early textiles only survive in a few parts of the world where the right conditions have existed to ensure preservation. However, some pieces produced in India have been found in other countries, indicating the scope of early textile trading throughout the Far and Middle East.

Much of the embroidery produced on the Indian subcontinent was made in the north-west – the River Indus plain and Thar desert area – where the first urban communities of that region started to develop some 2,000 years before the birth of Christ. The best-known sites are those at Harappa and Mohenjo-daro. The latter was a major trade and manufacturing centre with various workshops, including those of dyers and beadmakers. The cotton plant, which is indigenous to India, grew in the areas surrounding these cities. Embroidery may also have been well-advanced in this region, as among the finds is the bust of a man, who

1 *Bust of a priest-king, Mohenjo-daro, Indus Valley*
(NATIONAL MUSEUM, KARACHI, PAKISTAN)

appears to be a priest, wearing an ornate shawl (Figure 1). It has been suggested that the motifs on the shawl could have been worked in raised embroidery.

Illustrations in materials such as stone, which survive the ravages of time better than fabrics, give some idea of the appearance of textiles which disappeared long ago. Despite this evidence we can only guess at the techniques used in the making of a particular textile piece. Other finds from the fascinating site at Mohenjo-daro include a fragment of madder-dyed cotton fabric and some thin bronze needles.

There is other evidence that the existence of trade routes and the consequences of trading have had a considerable influence on Indian textiles.

2 *Cotton panel, embroidered with grass and silk. Glass was probably used, in a similar way to today's mirror work, but only pressure marks remain in the cloth. Fifteenth or sixteenth century. Jain, Gujarat*
(ACC. NO. 983. THE CALICO MUSEUM OF TEXTILES, AHMEDABAD)

Written accounts inform us that, as early as 300 BC, the wealthy peoples of this subcontinent wore richly embroidered clothes, and this coincides with the development of related skills and the use of similar products at this time in Egypt, Greece, Persia, Syria and Babylon. In the tenth century AD, slippers embroidered in gold and silver were exported from Sind (Pakistan) to Baghdad (Iraq). Many explorers documented their travels in some detail, and these accounts naturally add to our knowledge. The Venetian traveller Marco Polo visited India on his way back from China and referred to the exquisite embroideries made in Gujarat 'depicting birds and beasts in gold and silver thread sown [*sic*] very subtly on leather'. In early Chinese, Buddhist and Brahman writings, embroidery is often mentioned.

Unfortunately, there are comparatively few surviving examples of embroidery from before the Moghal period. The piece shown in Figure 2 is, perhaps, one of the oldest surviving Indian embroideries. It comes from the Gujarat and dates from the fifteenth or sixteenth century. There is a similar example of embroidery at the offices of AEDTA (Association pour l'Etude et la Documentation des Textiles d'Asie), in Paris, France.

Among the earliest Indian embroideries to be found in England are the seventeenth- (or possibly sixteenth-) century example at Hardwick Hall in Derbyshire, and the late seventeenth-century piece in the Victoria and Albert Museum in London. These are both valuable examples of the quality of early chain-stitch trade embroidery to come from the Gujarat. A great many of these chain-stitch embroideries were imported into Europe by the Dutch and English East India Companies. Figure 3 shows the central panel of a summer carpet, *c.* 1700, a superb example of high-quality embroidery. The stitching is very fine

3 *(Opposite) Moghal coverlet, central panel from a summer carpet, 137 x 102 cm (54 x 40 in), c.1700* (BERNHEIMER FINE ARTS LTD, LONDON)

4 *Satin stitch, showing both the face and reverse of the embroidery. Chinai, Surat, c.1900*

and exact, and the 'drawing' of the flowers, foliage and birds is highly controlled and skilful. It is embroidered in fine chain stitch in coloured silks, on a natural silk background which has a cotton backing; the stitching is through the two layers of fabric.

Naturally, examples from later periods are more common, and the European domination of India during the eighteenth and nineteenth centuries has meant that some fine collections of embroideries were built up and shipped to Europe.

In the Public Library at Preston, England, there are volumes of textile samples collected in India in the mid-1860s by Dr Forbes Watson. These were presented to the Town and Corporation of Preston by the Secretary of State for India (1866-72). To quote from the information on these volumes prepared by the Librarian:

'The volumes are from sets put together by Dr Forbes Watson in 1866 to 1872. They were intended to give British manufacturers examples of types of textiles for which there would be a market in India, so that they could copy and export them. The British manufacturers had the advantage of highly developed textile technology and so were able to flood the Indian market with cheap imitations which, unfortunately, had a detrimental effect on the native Indian textile industry.

100 sets of volumes were distributed in this country. Preston, as a textile-manufacturing town, received a set from the Secretary of State for India. India was at this time part of the British Empire.

A secondary intention was that the volumes should create a record of the wealth of Indian textiles of the period. They are now of great interest as they show not only the beauty and variety of nineteenth-century Indian textiles, but also record much information on the areas from which they came, the uses to which they were put and the names which were given.'

Some of the pieces from this collection can be seen in Figures 55 and 56 (page 69), 88 (page 100), 89 (page 101), 90 (page 102), 91(page 103), 95 (page 107) and 96 (page 108). The collection includes work created with a variety of techniques. Most of the embroidery examples come from Decca, Bengal (now Dhaka, Bangladesh), but some are from Hyderabad, Deccan and Madras. The embroidery was 'used in making women's bodices', 'for scarfs [sic] and head coverings' and 'to make up into scarfs'. Contemporary comments also tell us something of how the quality was regarded, such as 'a very fine example', or 'good quality'.

Similar examples of the embroideries housed in Preston, and from the same period, can be seen in the Victoria and Albert Museum in London and the Calico Museum in Ahmedabad, although these are not in book form.

5 *Black satin* aba *(wedding dress), embroidered with silk and very small mirror pieces. Nineteenth or twentieth century* (1929.121. LEWIS F. DAY COLLECTION, MANCHESTER CITY ART GALLERIES, GALLERY OF ENGLISH COSTUME, PLATT HALL)

6 *Detail of Figure 5*

Some of the settlers from other countries produced particular forms of embroidery, of which the type known as *chinai* is perhaps one of the best examples (see Figure 4). Some Chinese embroiderers settled during the nineteenth and twentieth centuries in Surat (north of Bombay) and made pieces of embroidery which would later be attached to saris and other garments.

Various ethnic groups make up the population of India today. This is a result of centuries of invasion by different peoples who settled and brought with them different religions, languages and skills. Religion has played an important part in the recent history of the subcontinent, when predominantly Muslim areas separated from mainly Hindu India to become Pakistan, and then Pakistan and Bangladesh (East Bengal). There were and still are many

religions practised in India, but it was the spread of the Moghal Empire to Delhi in the sixteenth century that brought the assimilation of Islamic influences with local styles into the large embroidery workshops set up by the rulers.

From this introduction, it can be seen that European influences, British control and trade with many countries have all had an influence on Indian embroidery.

Though certain stitches are common to all embroidery, local tradition has meant that regions have developed their own types and styles. The Muslim and Hindu religions have a powerful effect on the motifs and colours used in their work. Some embroidery processes are unique to India and, at times, the skill of the embroiderers and the overall standard of the workmanship has been superb. The practice of embroidery has not been restricted by caste and location, artefacts

7 *Shoemaker and embroiderer. Inscribed: 'shoemaker working with silk on cloth flowers, etc. Shoemaker. 18th. 19th.'*
(ADD. OR. 1539. BY PERMISSION OF THE BRITISH LIBRARY)

8 *Gold work and hook work being worked on frames, Lathfee Zari House, Madras, 1990. The workers sit in a comfortable position on the floor*

9 Anwer *embroidery, Madras, 1990. The embroiderer sits close to the frame so that he can use both hands easily to work above and below the frame*

being produced in a variety of techniques and materials, both for the rich at court and for the poor in the villages. As was the case in the past, specific techniques still generally relate to a particular region.

All the traditional skills and designs have by no means been lost, but the materials used may have changed; for instance, many man-made fabrics and threads are in use today. Each region still has its own identity, based on its dominant religion, patterns, cultural traditions and market requirements. The export trade – consumer-dictated – has harnessed the innate skill of the Indian craftsman, and techniques and styles have been adapted for foreign markets.

In 1948 the Indian government out-lawed the caste system, child marriage and other practices, which brought about a slow change in traditions. This has had some influence on the embroidery being made. As in other parts of the world, the rapid changes which have occurred during this century have meant that some techniques have died out, some are no longer used for their original purpose and others, sadly, have virtually disappeared.

Some areas have seen a recent revival of their traditional and local type of embroidery, as they have found that there is now a market for this work in the West. Co-operatives, development projects and workshops have been set up to help to centralize production and to create a marketing strategy for their embroidery. Sadly, much of this work is often not as well executed as it was

10 *Cobbler's* ari *with thread and ball of wax for stitching shoes, with part of finished leather embroidered shoe. Bhuj, Kutch, 1990*

worked directly on to the fabric from memory, or by looking at another piece of work. The design is often put on to the fabric, prior to embroidering, by a variety of methods. Sometimes an outline design is produced by block-printing. The pattern can also be created by tracing with a wooden pen or pencil. Stencilling on to cloth with coal dust (the 'prick-and-pounce' method) is also used, in which powdered clay or charcoal is

formerly, and much has been lost in the adoption of mass-production methods.

In India, textiles are everywhere: on clothes, adorning animals, in temples, homes and other buildings. These articles form part of the traditional way of life. Embroideries have been produced for many uses but, historically, the finest examples were largely produced for the courts and temples. Embroidery reached a professional status in the north and north-west, resulting in some exquisite workmanship, such as that produced by the Mochi and Banni peoples in the Kutch, Gujarat. An example can be seen in Figure 5, a detail of which is shown in Figure 6.

The stitches used have been determined largely by the fabrics available, and have also been dictated by the quality of the woven fabric. Interrelated with this has been the type of design to be worked: whether it is to be geometric and counted, or curved and free-flowing. The designs themselves are sometimes

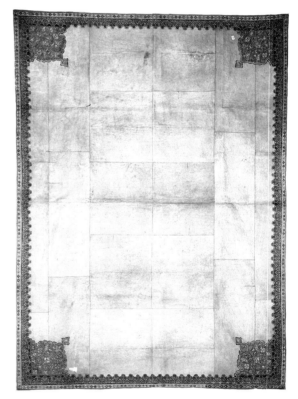

11 *Leather bedcover or horsecloth, 152 x 213 cm (60 x 84 in). The corner and border embroidery is worked on leather and applied to the pieced-leather background. Chain stitch. Gujarat, nineteenth century* (01973 [I M]. BY COURTESY OF THE BOARD OF TRUSTEES OF THE VICTORIA AND ALBERT MUSEUM, LONDON)

rubbed through perforated strong paper or copper foil.

Indian embroidery is usually worked on a single layer of fabric, but often the amount of stitching on the fabric necessitates another fabric being placed behind the first: this backing fabric is usually of an inferior quality to the one on the surface. Embroidery can be worked on a woven plain fabric, a woven patterned fabric or on pieces of different types of fabric, which have first been sewn together.

Most embroideries are worked in the hand, with the worker sitting in a comfortable position on the floor, as in the illustration in Figure 7. Some embroidery has to be worked on a tight fabric and, if this is the case, the fabric is stretched on a frame (similar to a slate frame) which is held off the ground at either end. This enables the embroiderer to sit close to the frame so that both hands can work above and below the frame with ease (Figures 8 and 9).

A wide variety of implements is used to enable these various techniques to be carried out. Naturally, there is also a wide variety in the sizes of needles, and some needles are specially made for certain processes. An example of this involves the needles for the pulled-thread *chikan* work (see pages 68–73), where the needle is fairly wide along its whole length. For some embroidery techniques involving metal threads, extra-long needles are used.

The *ari*, which can be seen in Figure 10, is a hooked awl and has been adapted over time to stitch embroidery designs on to leather, using different-sized hooks to accommodate the sizes of stitches and

12 *Sleeve band, Kashmir*
(1929.125. LEWIS F. DAY COLLECTION, MANCHESTER CITY ART GALLERIES, GALLERY OF ENGLISH COSTUME, PLATT HALL)

13 Chikan *embroiderer in Lucknow, 1990. The fabric she is stitching has been block-printed first*

types of thread. A piece produced by this method can be seen in Figure 11. The hooks are put into long, pencil-like holders for use on fabric that is stretched on a frame. The use of this technique is shown in Figure 106 on page 117. These hooks are very like the tambour hooks used in Europe. The constant use of the needles means that they have a working life of perhaps only twelve days before needing to be sharpened or replaced. The hooks are now made from any suitable metal that is available, including umbrella spokes. Threads are normally cut with scissors, but if these are not available a piece of glass is used.

The most commonly used background fabric is woven cotton, though some silks and wool are also used. Cotton fabrics have been woven in India since prehistoric times and, occasionally, the weaving has been so fine that it was called 'woven air'. The embroidery on this fabric is of the highest quality. The knowledge of silk and silk-weaving is assumed to have reached India from China. It is thought that the use of wild silk occurred in about the third century BC, and that of cultivated silk not before the first century AD. Wool and other hair fibres are local materials produced in areas where goats and sheep are raised.

Embroidery threads of cotton, silk, wool, silver and gold are often identical to those used in weaving. In fact, they are sometimes obtained by extracting the threads from an existing woven fabric. The colours used for the fabrics and embroidery are varied. The brightest and most dominant are seen in the arid and desert regions, particularly in the states of Gujarat and Rajasthan. The women wearing these brightly coloured embroidered garments have been called 'the flowers of the desert'.

Traditional and similar patterns, motifs and images are used in many art-and-craft forms, and similar patterns and imagery are often seen in the textile arts of weaving, printing and embroidery. Embroidery depicting a group of musicians, worked on a sleeve-band, is shown in Figure 12. The style is similar to that used in miniature paintings.

Sometimes a block-printer may print a design on to cloth for the embroiderer to use as a guide. Figure 13 shows a woman working on this type of printed cloth. With typical ingenuity, the same block can be used to produce a printed pattern on its own.

The approach to embroidery stitches in India is rather different from that in Europe. Many stitches are worked with the back, or reverse, of the work facing the embroiderer, as the back is often important too, and the embroidery there-fore becomes reversible. The embroiderer does not merely think of embellishing the existing fabric, but works more like a weaver, for whom the decorative element is intrinsic to the construction of the piece. Perhaps this should not be surprising, as the embroidery often arises from – or imitates – a woven piece and uses the same threads. Some of the techniques involve the use of one stitch only; for example, the running stitch in *kantha* work. It is the inventive way in which the stitch, thread and fabric are used which makes it into such a distinctive technique. It would therefore seem appropriate that, not only are the stitches used in Indian embroidery recognized, but also that the following points are observed:

1 the shapes made by the stitches
2 the negative shapes achieved in the unworked areas of the fabric
3 the size and spacing of the stitches
4 the types of fabrics and threads used
5 the combination of stitches used together in a particular piece

It is the imaginative use and combination of embroidery stitches which often makes Indian embroideries so remarkable and so worthy of study.

An important factor governing the appearance of the stitches is the way in which they have been worked. Some writers have observed that Indian embroiderers stitch away from themselves, in the opposite direction to that employed in Europe; others dispute this statement. It is my opinion, from observation and analysis of work, that the former method is the most common. It does not appear possible to produce the piece shown on page 11, for example, with the chain stitch made so evenly with a needle, unless it is worked away from the embroiderer. This direction is maintained whenever possible, and the fabric can be turned in the hand to facilitate this. A young man working in this fashion can be seen in Figure 14. If the embroidery is on a large frame, however, (see Figure 8 on page 15), it is obviously not possible to turn the fabric. Chain stitch, which is worked on a frame, is likely to be carried out with a hook (tambour or *ari*) rather than with a regular needle.

14 *Embroiderer stitching in Pipli, Orissa, 1990*

Over a period of time new stitches and designs have been added to those traditionally used, and these have also been adapted and changed. Often, old designs have been augmented and changed, and have evolved to a point where they are barely recognizable from the original. An example of this is the design of the green parrot, a common bird in parts of India. In Figure 66 on page 80, for instance, the birds on either side of the large circular motifs are simple 'S' shapes. These are still recognizable, but mainly because they have been used in this position on similar embroideries.

In the past, and in India today, stitches and designs are often passed on from mother to daughter. In this way, some of the techniques and designs have remained largely the same, with gradual changes occurring with an embroiderer improvising or adding an individual touch. When time allowed, embroidery was traditionally made by women in the villages and was entered into as part of an enjoyable social gathering. The main occupation in the villages centred on agriculture, so there was time during the seasons to have such gatherings. Today there are still fewer distractions in areas where development and modernization have yet to change the way in which the village people spend their leisure time. This embroidery is for the family, home and community.

In recent years, the people of the villages have been encouraged to use their embroidery skills to supplement their income from agriculture, which is of course reliant on the vagaries of the climate. The co-operatives set up to produce work for sale at home and abroad are helping to keep people on the land and to slow migration to the over-crowded cities. The drop in quality resulting from this type of organization is by no means universal.

Embroidery is still produced by professional embroiderers and, in general, it is the men who are involved in this kind of work. A very rigid method of working and training has evolved. Often a master embroiderer trains others by passing on the process and the manipulative skills for a particular form of work, and this is frequently in a father-and-son relationship. This continuity of training ensures quality regulation, but it does not imply that controlled, quality work is *only* produced by these professional embroiderers. The same control can still be seen in the work of the nomadic Banjara peoples, for instance, who produce the most delicate and even stitching. Their method is to stitch from the bottom of a piece, gradually working up to the top, as if working from the earth to the sky, and so representing the whole universe in their embroidery. Some motifs appear to have lost their symbolic meaning, but are, nevertheless, still embroidered.

1

Embroidery stitches

As a result of the differing historical developments in various regions of India, it is not surprising that the embroidery stitches used differ between distinct communities. Having said this, the same stitches are often used in different communities, but are frequently adapted in different ways to produce individual motifs, and are used for a variety of purposes. With improved mobility, however, communities are increasingly 'borrowing' or assimilating motifs and stitches from each other.

Stitches introduced from other countries by invaders and settlers have been absorbed into local work and have changed or developed over a period of time. For example, chain stitch was probably introduced to west Gujarat (to what is now called Kutch) from Baluchistan (now part of Pakistan), and is thought originally to have come from further west. Chain stitch and satin stitch may well have come to other parts of India from China. Chain stitch is rarely used for embroidery in China today, but examples of it have been found in ancient tombs.

The stitches discussed in this chapter are all made by hand with a needle or *ari* (awl or tambour hook; see Figure 10 on page 16). Chain stitch can also be produced on a Cornely machine and one has to look carefully to see the method used for each embroidery. The stitches fall into the following groups: herring-bone (and interlaced) stitches, feather stitches, fly stitches, cretan, buttonhole, chain, straight (including unrelated-line) stitches, couchings, stem stitches, running and back stitches, cross stitches, single-unit stitches, edgings and filling stitches. See pages 137–40 for diagrams of how to work the stitches described here and throughout the book.

In the samples illustrated, the face and reverse of the stitches are shown to help identification. When learning how to complete a stitch, and to check that it is correct, it is a help to look at the back as well as the front. The examples show how stitches are used in a particular way; often, very ordinary stitches are used to great effect. To understand the techniques fully, copying a section of embroidery will give you a clear idea of the methods

15 Rumal. *Plain-weave, embroidered, painted and block-printed by hand, 55·9 x 55·6 cm (22 x 21¾ in). Himachal Pradesh, Chamba, India. Nineteenth century*
(ACC. NO. 58.2-107, ELIZABETH BAYLEY WILLIS COLLECTION, HENRY ART GALLERY, UNIVERSITY OF WASHINGTON)

16 *(Right) Detail of Figure 15*

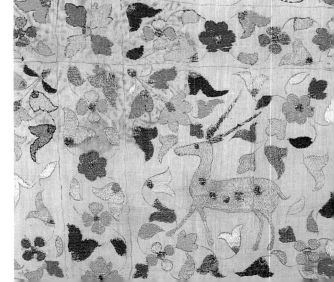

used. This should be done with similar materials and tools to those used in the original. With a closely woven fabric, sharp-pointed needles are used; with an open-weave fabric the needle is usually a blunted one.

It is difficult to isolate embroidery stitches, as they are often used in combination with other techniques. The stitches illustrated in this chapter are also shown in other chapters with specific techniques.

Examples have been chosen from different states of India to show how stitches are used to fill shapes, to make shapes, to create patterns and to leave negative shapes, using different types of fabric

17 Rumal. *Plain-weave, embroidered, 71 cm (28 in) square. Himachal Pradesh, Chamba, India, nineteenth century*
(ACC. NO. 58.2-112, ELIZABETH BAYLEY WILLIS COLLECTION, HENRY ART GALLERY, UNIVERSITY OF WASHINGTON)

and thread and different-sized stitches. Some pieces are worked all in one stitch; others use a number of stitches in the same piece. Some are on one piece of cloth, on pieced cloths or on layers of cloth. Stitches are worked with either the back or the face of the embroidery toward the worker. The stitches are familiar to all embroiderers, but their uses and the methods of working them are particular to Indian embroidery.

The square and oblong *rumals* shown in Figures 15, 16 and 17 are embroidered covers and decorative pieces, and are thought to have originated during the eighteenth century in Chamba (in the state of Himachal Pradesh). They are influenced by the painted miniatures of

18 Kangra *painting, eighteenth century. Brihmkumaries offering food to Lord Krishna. The offerings are covered with embroidered* rumals (S.M.L. **48.49.** STATE MUSEUM, LUCKNOW)

the Moghal courts and probably originated when this area was a thriving artistic centre. They continued to be made up to the early part of this century. They are often described as paintings translated into embroidery. Figure 18 shows caskets covered with embroidered *rumals*.

The *rumals* vary technically, and some are influenced by the *phulkari* technique (see pages 55–67). The main stitches in Figures 15, 16 and 17 are cross stitch, double-running stitch, buttonhole stitch, long and short stitch, pattern-darning

19 *Bodice front. Kutch, Gujarat, 1980s* (COLLECTION MEIRA STOCKL)

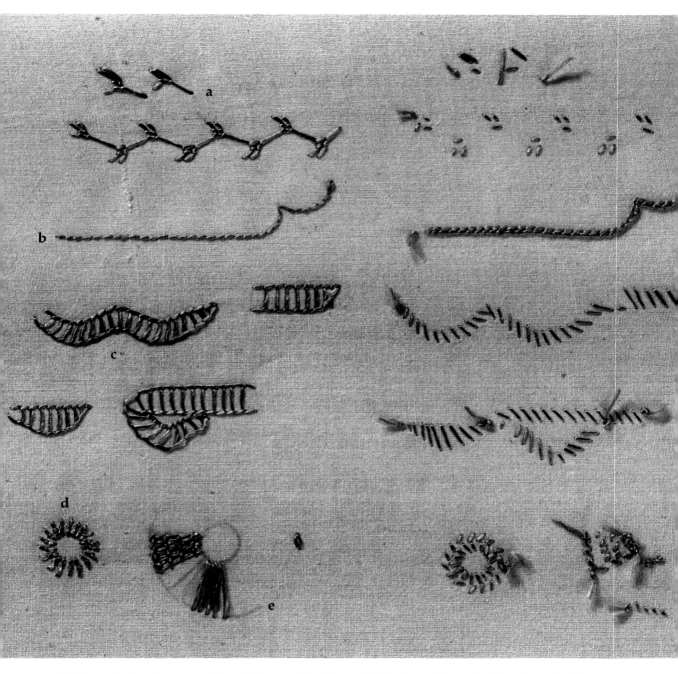

20 *Sample showing some of the stitches used in Figure 19. The face of the embroidery is on the left, the reverse on the right*

21 *Detail of a cover. Kutch, Gujarat, 1985*

21a *This detail of Figure 21 emphasizes the way in which the white, unstitched areas are a key element in the design*

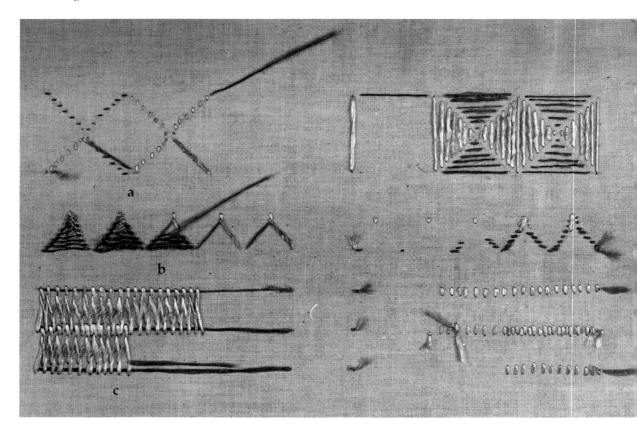

22 *Darning and cretan stitches over a base thread. This sample shows the way these stitches have been used in Figure 21*

and herringbone stitch. The designs will have been drawn on to the fabric with fine charcoal by the artist/designer, who probably also decided the colours, with the embroiderer working to the given guidelines.

In Figure 19, an example from Gujarat, pieces of cotton fabric have been sewn together to produce a background fabric of different colours. Another piece of fabric has been placed behind, so that the embroidery is stitched through two layers. The stitches used are mirror work, reverse chain, open chain, double chain (mainly worked to fill shapes), double-tied cretan, laid work (tied horizontally with a couched line, or sometimes with a line of reverse chain stitch) and Romanian stitch (also known as Indian filling stitch).

Figure 20 shows some of the stitches used in the piece in Figure 19. They are: (a) double-tied cretan stitch (b) reverse chain stitch (c) open chain stitch (d) Romanian stitch and (e) laid work, tied horizontally. Of particular note is the way the double-tied cretan stitch is used as a line or as a little mark, and the way the open chain stitch is angled and narrowed to form wavy lines, to turn corners or to make a shape. For reverse chain stitch, the embroiderer has turned the piece over and worked a line of chain stitch so that the reverse shows on the face as a controlled, dotted line. Romanian stitch and laid work form the circular shapes.

Figure 21, another example from Gujarat, is created from a single piece of fabric which has been embroidered in one colour so that the negative shapes left by the stitching create shapes in the background fabric. From a distance it is these unworked areas which have the major visual impact (see opposite).

Figure 22 illustrates some of the stitches used in the piece in Figure 21. These have been worked on both sides of the cloth, showing the influence of *phulkari*. The darning stitch is worked in squares to form a diamond and half-diamond border with the reverse side facing the worker (a). This method makes it much easier for the embroiderer to count the warp and weft threads of the base fabric, so that a regular border of stitches is formed on the other side. In (b) and (c) the cretan stitches show how a thread is put down first (single cretan, straight line), which draws the design on to the fabric and also raises the cretan stitch from the fabric. The cretan stitch is worked over this base stitch to form shapes or rows.

Figures 23 and 24, and the detail in Figure 25, show the fine work produced in Kashmir. They illustrate the way in which the stitches make motifs, borders and fabrics of solid stitching (that is, with no background fabric showing).

Traditionally, it is thought that this type of embroidery developed when the menders of woven shawls, who re-created worn parts by joining pieces invisibly, were asked to stitch the entire shawl. These embroidered shawls even copied the texture and twill weave of the originals. Very few old pieces survive, but those from the late nineteenth century and early twentieth century have very fine stitching. The designs were put on to the cloth through perforated parchment (later, thick paper); coal dust was rubbed through the holes and then the outline was heightened with a pen, ready for the embroidery to be worked.

The woven-and-embroidered-shawl technique developed at the end of the nineteenth century. The embroidery could be stitched so that the shawl was double-sided, or stitched through just half of the fabric so that the design was seen only on one side with nothing showing on the reverse. This latter method was sometimes used to create a double-sided embroidery with different colours on either side. The fabric and thread were usually fine wool, with the stitching making a soft addition to the fabric. The intricate build-up of fine, spiky stitches is only visible through a magnifier, and the effect is very delicate.

The main stitches are split stitch, forms of Romanian stitch, buttonhole and stem stitch (often whipped), satin stitch, single fly stitch, outline stitch and running stitch. The combinations of these stitches with fine thread on a small scale prevents any single stitch from standing out. The whole works together with a subtle use of colours.

Figure 23 shows details from two shawls. Here the embroidery is used to make borders, motifs and an all-over pattern which leaves very little of the background fabric unworked.

The prayer mat in Figure 24 (a detail is shown in Figure 25) illustrates the same intricacy and care for stitches and colour when the embroidery is on a large-scale work, completely covering the back-ground fabric. Figure 12 on page 17 shows another example of a Kashmiri embroidery.

In Figure 26, two forms of stem stitch are shown at (a) and (b). Split stitch is

shown at (c) and types of Romanian stitch at (d). Fly stitch is shown forming a pattern at (e), and whipped stem stitch and a form of fly stitch at (f). Buttonhole is held down by a small stitch at (g) and satin stitch forms a shape at (h). Buttonhole stitch makes a pattern at (i) and two lines of stem stitch (with a satin stitch in the middle) are shown at (j). This sample shows some of the stitches and some of the ways in which they are put together. The scale is much larger than the Indian originals, but gives some idea of the detailing involved in this kind of embroidery.

The embroidered bag in Figure 27, which comes from the Deccan, illustrates the effective use of running stitch and interlaced running stitch. It is made of three layers of cotton fabric, the edges turned under and held together with small and large running stitches. The smaller stitches form bands between the areas where the larger stitches form the base for interlacing patterns.

Figure 28 shows some of the interlaced stitches used in Figure 27, at (a) and (b). Chain stitch is sometimes used as the base, as shown at (c) and (d). The running stitches are worked in different directions but always in a brick pattern; alternating rows are the same.

The three examples in Figure 29, from Gujarat and Rajasthan, show various uses of herringbone stitch. The top piece shows the use of herringbone stitch as a foundation, which is then interlaced with

23 (*Opposite*) *Details from two shawls. Kashmir, late twentieth century*
(COLLECTION OF RAVINDER SINGH)

a thread. This technique is shown in Figure 30 at (e), (g) and (h). The piece in the centre incorporates diamond shapes produced by the technique shown in Figure 22(a) on page 28. The other effects in this piece are produced by using the stitches shown in Figure 30 at (a) and (f). The lower piece is made as shown in Figure 30 at (f). The centre and lower pieces illustrate the clever ways in which one type of stitch (in this case herringbone) can be used to create quite different effects. In the lower piece the stitch is used to cover the background fabric completely. It is worked in blocks and developed in a diagonal manner. In the

24 *(Opposite) Prayer mat. Kashmir* (1929.118, LEWIS F. DAY COLLECTION, MANCHESTER CITY ART GALLERIES, GALLERY OF ENGLISH COSTUME, PLATT HALL)

25 *Detail of Figure 24*

centre piece the stitch is used to create blocks, leaving parts of the background visible to produce interesting negative shapes.

The worked samples in Figure 30 show a simple herringbone stitch at (a), a threaded herringbone stitch at (b), and a herringbone stitch held with two rows of running stitch at (c). Two rows of herringbone worked on top of each other and then held down with three rows of running stitch are shown at (d), interlaced herringbone stitch at (e), and diagonal blocks of close herringbone at (f). The stitching at (g) produces a broad band of interlaced herringbone stitch, and (h) shows Maltese cross stitch.

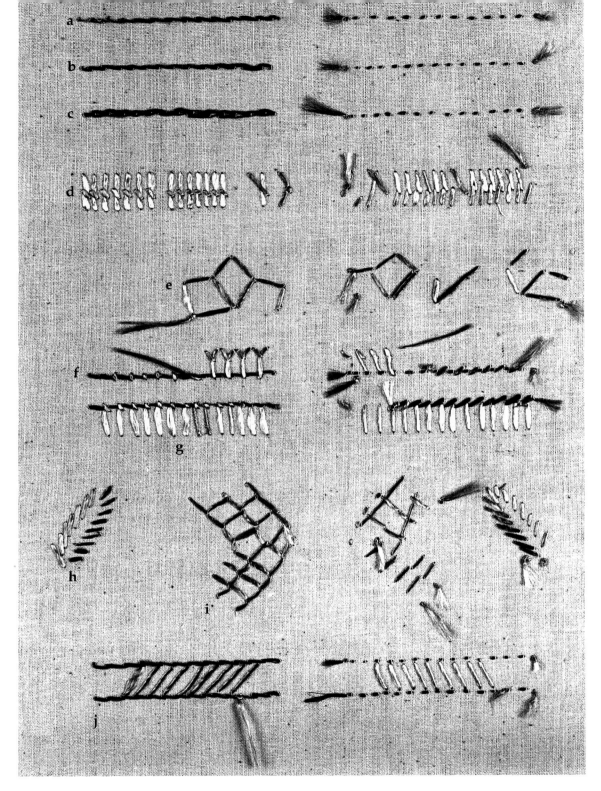

26 *Sample showing stitches used in Kashmiri embroidery. The face of the embroidery is on the left, the reverse on the right*

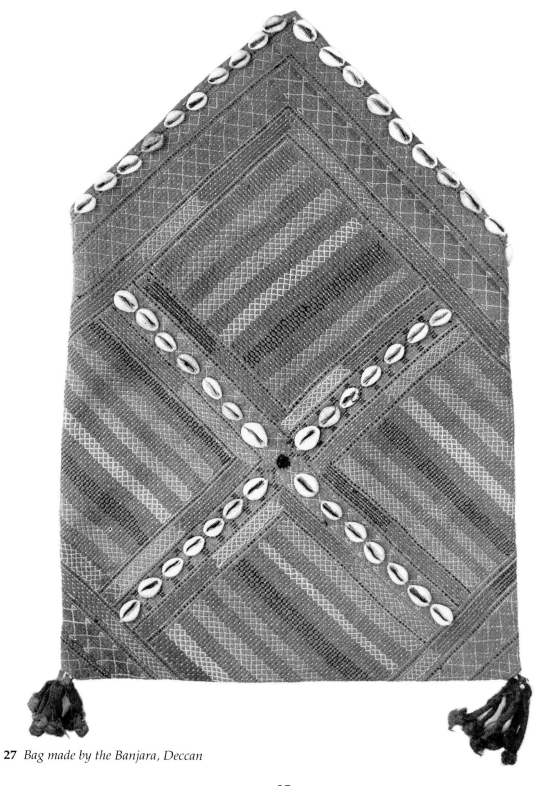

27 *Bag made by the Banjara, Deccan*

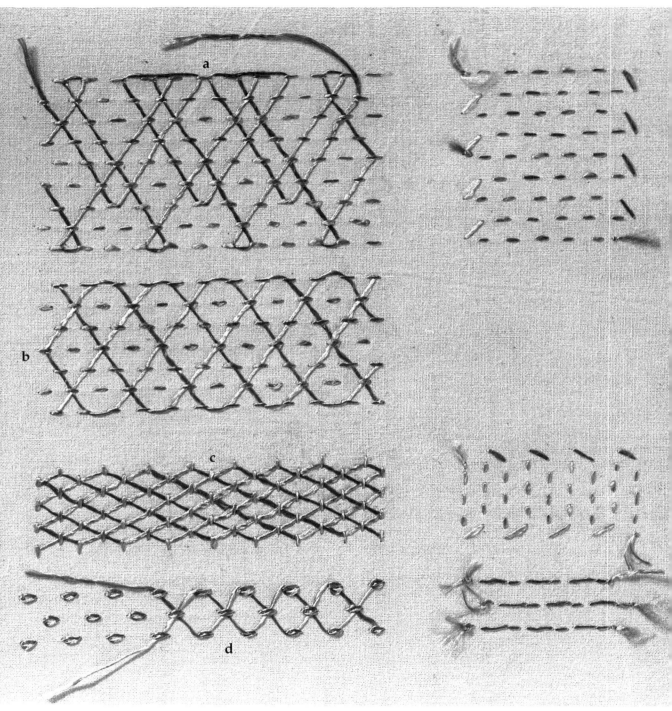

28 *Sample showing four interlaced patterns on a running-stitch and chain-stitch base. The face of the embroidery is on the left, the reverse on the right*

29 *(Opposite) Details of embroidered fabrics from Gujarat and Rajasthan*

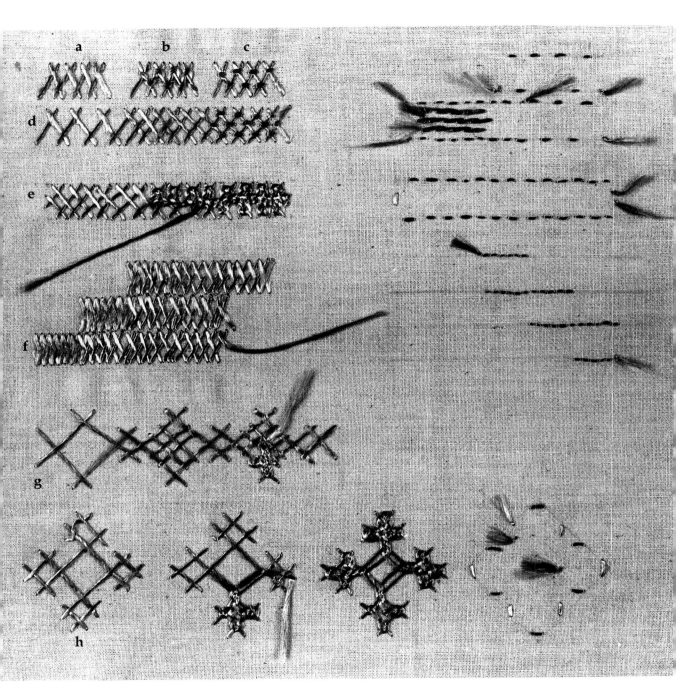

30 *Sample of different herringbone stitches. The face of the work is on the left, the reverse on the right*

2

Quilting, darning and pattern-darning

Quilting is an embroidery technique in which two or three fabrics are sewn together to make a warm, and also often decorative, fabric. The process makes a whole from pieces of discarded fabric and rags, and is a very effective way of recycling old and worn fabrics (see Figure 31).

Different approaches to quilting have developed in different communities to produce varied uses of stitches, patterns and designs. In India there are three areas which create distinct quilting styles: Gujarat, West Bengal and Bihar. The common element of the work from these areas is that, traditionally, they all use discarded, worn fabrics. However, this is not the case today in the villages and co-operatives where pieces are produced using new fabrics for tourists, trade and export. A range of sizes is made for various uses, such as bedspreads and other covers.

In the Gujarat, old fabrics (often from clothes) are put together to form quilts,

and two examples of this work can be seen in Figures 32 and 34. The usual number of layers is two, although sometimes it can be three. To make a large piece of fabric, smaller pieces are first sewn together. If you look closely at Figure 32, the joins in the fabric can be seen, although Figure 31, which shows everyday quilts being aired, perhaps reveals this more clearly.

The layers are first held together with spirals and triangles (Figure 33), or sometimes angled oblongs or zigzags are used. Once the background has been secured together in this way, various motifs, some depicting local scenes, are embroidered in an apparently random fashion. The border is then added, usually in contrasting fabric(s), which in turn is sewn, and often embroidered, with various embroidery stitches and appliqué. This can be seen in the quilt in Figure 34. The edge of this quilt has been applied and stitched, and embroidered with mirror work, buttonhole and

31 *Everyday quilts put out to air. Bhuj, Gujarat, 1990*

32 *Quilted fabric, 122 x 164 cm (48 x 64½ in)*   **33** *(Opposite) Quilting shapes from Figure 32*

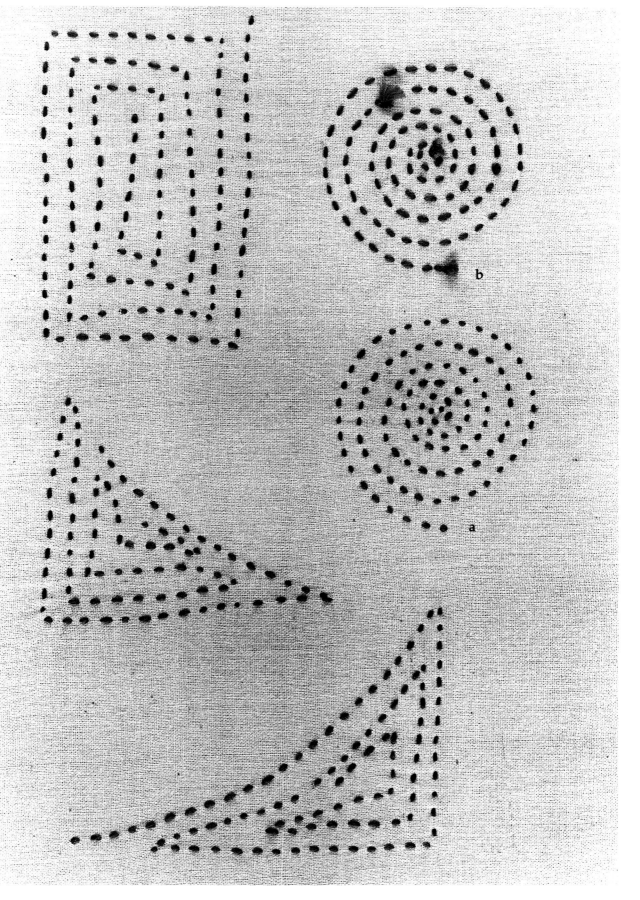

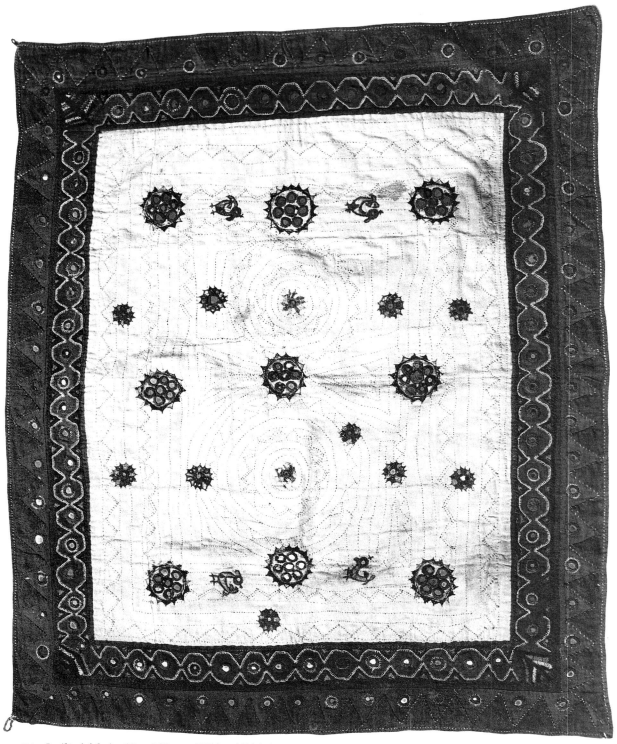

34 *Quilted fabric, 85 x 103 cm (33½ x 40½ in)*

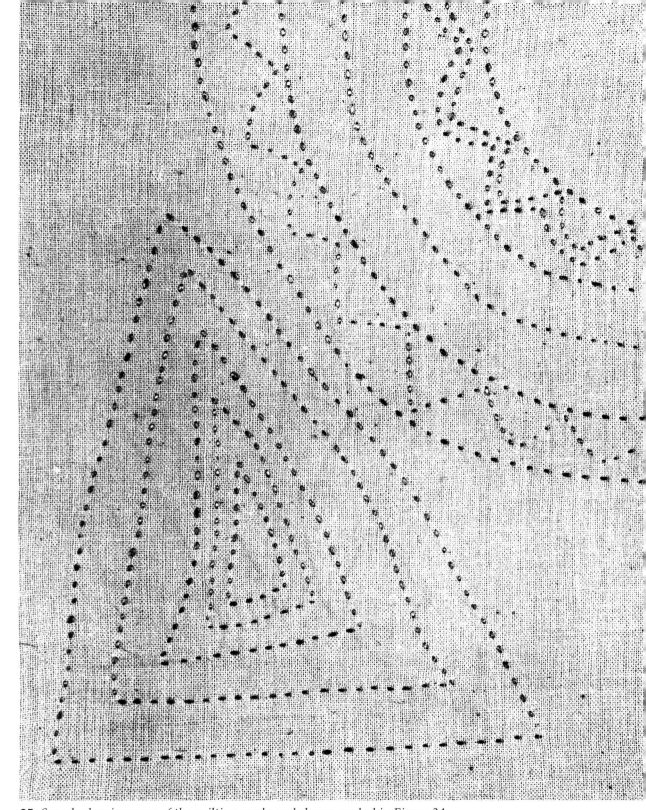

35 *Sample showing some of the quilting marks and shapes worked in Figure 34*

herringbone stitches. The centre has been embroidered with herringbone stitch in the manner of the samples worked in Figure 22 at (b) and (c) on page 28. Chain stitch and mirror work have also been added.

The edge of the quilt in Figure 32 has been applied and stitched in the technique demonstrated in Figure 120 on page 134. The embroidery has been carried out in herringbone stitch, mirror work and chain stitch. The design has been outlined first and embroidered as shown in Figure 22(b) and (c) on page 28.

In the two worked examples shown in Figures 33 and 35, the running stitch (which is quilting the fabrics together) is worked so that the reverse side is facing the embroiderer during stitching – another example of the influence of the *phulkari* approach (see pages 55–67). The samples are worked through two layers of fabric. In Figure 33, (a) shows the side of the stitching which becomes the 'right' or face side, while (b) shows the stitching which becomes the 'wrong' or reverse side of the fabric (the side facing the worker when stitching).

Figures 36 and 37 show details of quilts. These types of quilt, named *kantha*, are made in Bengal, now India (West Bengal) and Bangladesh (East Bengal). They were worked by women in their leisure time, and unfortunately no pieces made before the mid-nineteenth century are thought to survive. The fabric used is discarded cloth, usually from worn-out cotton saris; the thicker the cotton or number of layers, the coarser the embroidery. To keep the layers uniform and straight, weights are placed on the four corners. The four

sides are tacked through the layers, and then, in selected places, the three layers are stitched to keep them in position.

The threads used for the embroidery – white and colours – are taken from the woven border of the base fabric. These are then used for stitching and embroidery. Close running stitches darn the pieces together so that the join is almost invisible. In the main, the white thread is used on the background and the coloured threads to make the design, motifs and border pattern.

The stitching starts in the middle of the quilt and is worked outwards. In the past, the design was worked from memory, but today the motifs are usually marked out prior to stitching (some examples show this to be either with a pencil or ballpoint pen). The background is stitched in a series of small blocks, worked in different directions. When stitched, the *kantha* has a rippled effect.

The quilt can be worked with an evenly spaced stitch, so that it is identical on either side, or worked with a long stitch on the side facing the embroiderer and a short stitch on the reverse. This latter method gives a dotted look to the stitching. Woven patterns taken from sari borders are reproduced by long and short running stitches and often form a border round the quilt. One of these patterns can be seen at the lower edge of the detail shown in Figure 37. The samples worked in in Figure 38 show how the running stitch is used as an outline for the motifs and also to create the motif itself. The development is shown from (a) to (f).

Much of the symbolism is religious in origin, taken from Buddhism, Hinduism

36 *Detail of* Kantha *quilt, this section 43 x 33 cm (17 x 13 in). Bengal, early twentieth century*
(COLLECTION OF JOHN GILLOW)

and Islam. Other symbolism is based on local folk art, scenes of village life, scenes from the East India Company, and symbolic motifs such as the three elements: earth, fire and water.

Another type of quilting is *sujani*, which is normally used for bedcovers. An example of this work is shown in Figure 39, a quilt from Bihar. As with the *kantha*, fabrics from old saris and dhotis are used. The white background fabric is first stitched with a running stitch of the same colour as the background fabric, as shown in Figure 42 at (c). Four layers of fabric are held together with a running stitch, and the whole piece is stitched in this way before anything else is done to the fabric. The lines of running stitch are worked in straight lines from one end of the fabric to the other. The line starts with a knot and finishes with a knot, and these remain visible on the back of the work.

The stitching on top of this preparatory work is mainly a darning stitch which, apart from the start and finish of the thread, is only stitched through the top layer of fabric. Figure 40 is a sample showing the lines of quilting, the darning stitch (just catching the fabric and giving an appearance similar to couching) and chain stitch. The darning stitch can also be seen in Figure 42 at (d), where a single line of the stitch is used, and at (e), where three lines are used. The darning stitch on the surface, which fills the motifs, is worked through the top layer of fabric

37 *Detail of* Kantha *quilt, this section 23 x 18 cm (9 x 7 in). West Bengal, 1987*

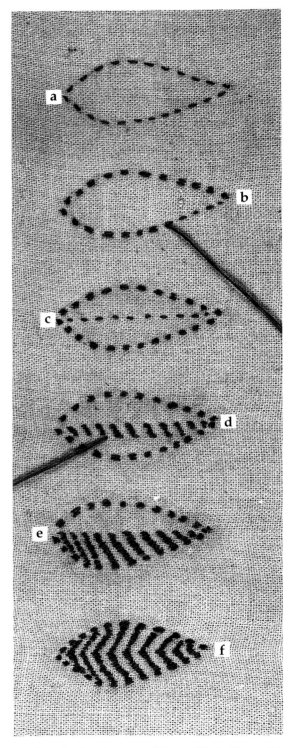

38 *Sample showing one of the motifs in Figure 37*

39 Sujani *quilt from Bihar, 124 x 219 cm (49 x 86 in)*

40 *Sample of the quilting lines, surface darning and chain stitch used in the quilt in Figure 39*

41 *Detail of an embroidered cloth, this section
31 x 38 cm (12 x 15 in). Bengal, early twentieth
century* (COLLECTION OF JOHN GILLOW)

42 *(Opposite) Samples of stitches and quilting.
The face of the work is on the left, the reverse on
the right*

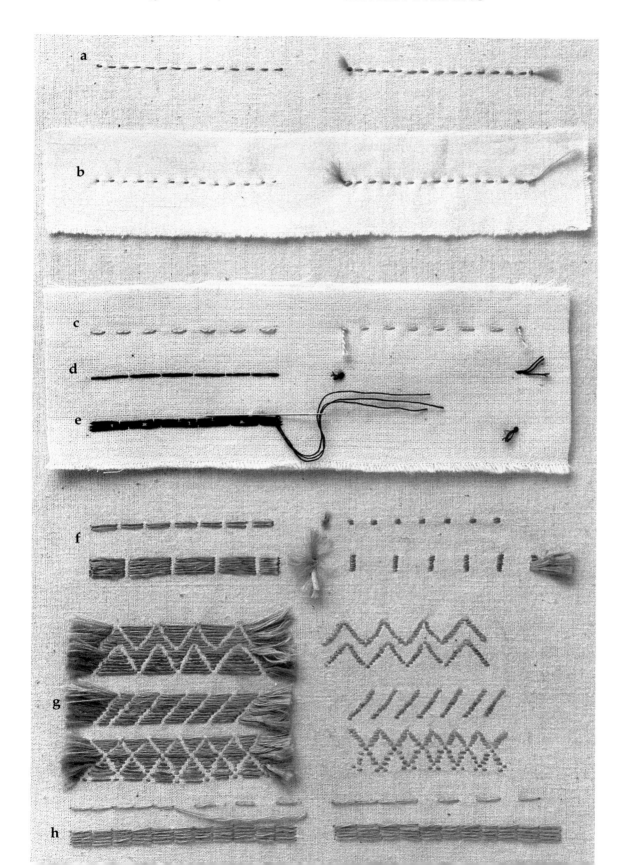

only and so does not appear on the reverse side. Sometimes, chain or herring-bone stitches are used to make lines and outlines, and these are worked through all the layers of cloth. Some of the shapes are made in one colour; others in two colours. The shapes are worked from the centres out towards the edges, so that, when a piece is worked in two colours, the shape is divided.

The border on the quilt in Figure 39 shows a series of applied coloured fabrics, held down to the top layer with a running stitch in a self-colour.

Some of the types of stitches found in quilting can be seen in Figure 41. These include darning, pattern-darning and patterns with long and short stitches. This is a fine example of the patterns which can be achieved with a darning stitch. This example, a detail of a larger piece, is worked in cotton thread on cotton fabric. The darning stitch shown in Figure 42 at (d) and (e) is really a long running stitch, in which a small amount of fabric is picked up with the needle between each stitch; in Figure 41 this can be seen outlining the motifs and figures.

The shapes made by the darning stitch are filled with pattern-darning, as in Figure 42(f). Here the small amount of fabric is picked up with the needle and worked in several rows which make a pattern in themselves. The border of leaves shows various patterns, and the bodices and trousers of the seated female figures are stitched so that on one there is a zigzag pattern and on the other a diamond pattern.

The bands of patterns which divide up areas in this type of embroidery are made with long and short running stitches. These are usually carried out in a strict method, which involves counting the threads of the warp and weft of the background fabric so that the pattern is exact. In this example, however, the fabric is a very close weave, so the 'counting' has been done by eye. The first few rows of stitching are carefully counted, after which it is not necessary to count as the stitching follows naturally. These patterns are taken from woven patterns on the borders of saris, and can also be seen in *kantha* quilts.

Figure 42 shows a running stitch through one layer of fabric at (a), through two layers at (b) and through four layers at (c). A single line of darning stitch has been worked at (d), three lines at (e) and a sample of pattern-darning at (f). Some examples of darned patterns are shown at (g) and rows of double running stitch at (h). The latter is called double darning when used as a filling rather than as a line of stitching.

Similar pattern-darning on woven white-cotton shawls is used by the Todas of Ootacamund in the Nilgiri hills. The end of the shawl has woven bands and the patterns are embroidered by the women alongside the bands and in blocks. The patterns are worked to appear woven, the threads are the same as those used for the weaving and the patterns are embroidered with a similar tension. They are stitched backwards and forwards with a continuous thread.

3
Counted-thread work

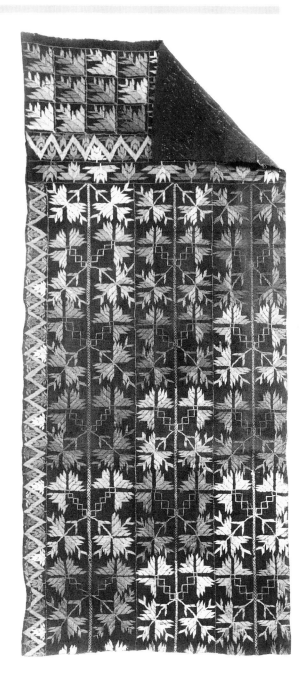

There are different kinds of counted-thread work in various parts of India, in particular in the Punjab, Rajasthan, Gujarat, Bihar, Karnataka and the Deccan, where the Banjara travel.

One of the major types of counted-thread work is generally known as *phulkari*, meaning 'flowering work'. It is worked by women, often in groups, and is produced in northern India, especially in the Punjab. Little of this work is produced today, but its influence can be seen in other kinds of embroidery. The technique is thought to date back at least to the fifteenth century and could have been introduced from central Asia by migrating tribes. The designs are mainly geometric patterns, although some are freer and include animals, flowers and, more recently, railway trains and other images of modern life. The geometric patterns symbolize fields, crops and various objects owned by the family. There are many types of *phulkari* designs:

43 Phulkari *worked on four strips of fabric. The edge is turned back to show the reverse side. 125 x 257 cm (49 x 101 in). Punjab, early twentieth century*

44 *Detail of a phulkari. Punjab, early twentieth century*

some in a distinct style and others in a combination of styles; some very simple and sparsely embroidered and others heavily embroidered. The designs were passed from generation to generation and samplers were used for this purpose. A study of these samplers shows how the patterns have evolved and changed.

There are four main categories and today they are all referred to as *phulkari*. *Bagh* is the name given to the kind of *phulkari* in which little of the background fabric shows through; the fabric is embroidered with patterns in a darning stitch which almost covers the whole surface. Examples of this work can be seen in Figures 43 and 44. In the type known as *chope*, the embroidery is often worked only at the sides of a length of cloth and is made with a double running stitch which is identical on both sides of the fabric. An example of this is shown in Figure 45. Figure 46 shows a type of *phulkari* known as *sainchi*. This is the name given to work when figures are included. The fourth type is called *shishadar* or *sheesh bagh*. This name is used when *shisha* (mirrors) are included, an example of which is shown in Figure 47.

Designs are embroidered from memory, often after having studied older pieces. To help start the design, the first parts to be stitched are marked by scoring the fabric with a needle, or the main design is tacked out (or a running stitch used). Soft rubbing is another method, in which designs are rubbed on to the fabric using an existing embroidery, on which the fabric to be embroidered is placed. Then a metal pot, smeared with a little hair oil, is rubbed over the surface to produce an

45 *Detail of a* phulkari. *The edge is turned back to show that the back is the same as the front. Early twentieth century*
(COLLECTION OF DR CHAN SANDHU)

embossed pattern on the fabric. The designs are worked from bottom to top and back again, or sometimes from side to side. The background is usually an even-weave cotton cloth, dyed to an earth-red rusty colour or indigo blue. The usual *phulkari* shawl size is about 1·5 x 2·5 m (5 x 8 ft), so the pieces are worked in separate panels and then sewn together to make the finished piece. *Phulkari* shawls were made for weddings and festivals, and this form of embroidery was also used on everyday clothes. The

46 Phulkari *from the Punjab or Haryana, embroidered with figures and folk motifs.*
One of the many pieces stored in the home, 1890 to 1930 (COLLECTION OF MR WAZIL)

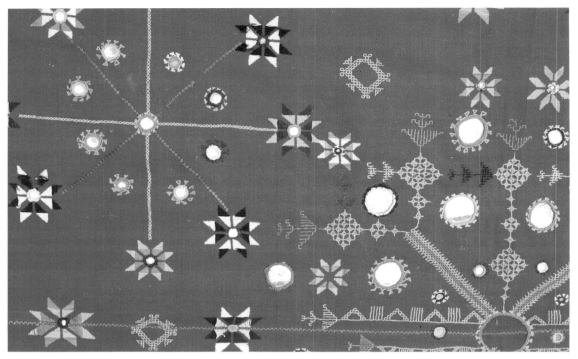

shawl was used after the ceremony as a wallhanging or bedcover.

Darning stitch in *phulkari* is usually started with a small knot or back stitch and finished with a little back stitch. The embroidery is worked with the reverse side of the cloth, which faces the worker. The stitches change direction, and this, combined with the use of an untwisted, soft-floss silk thread, reflects the light, giving the surface a shiny appearance. The traditional colours of thread would include white, gold, orange, green and crimson.

Figure 48 shows the usual way in which a motif is worked in four sections. One section of vertical and horizontal lines, or darning stitch, is worked to make a quarter of the motif. Some motifs, however, are stitched entirely in a vertical darning stitch. Each section in this motif is worked from the central

47 *Detail of an embroidered head cover from the Rajasthan/Madhya Pradesh border. Early twentieth century*
(COLLECTION OF MR WAZIL)

lines out to the edge of the motif, i.e., the first line started at (a) and finished at (b), the next line started at (c) and finished at (d), and so on. The rest of the illustration shows the work as it looks when being stitched, with this side facing the worker (the long threads are on the other side). This method enables the embroiderer to count the threads of the cloth more easily.

Double-running-stitch *phulkari* is started without a knot, the first stitch being locked in by the final stitch, as shown in Figure 49 at (b). The embroidery is worked face-up to the worker and is reversible. The double running stitches, shown in Figure 42(h) on

48 *Sample of darning stitch. The top-left corner shows the side facing the worker when stitching*

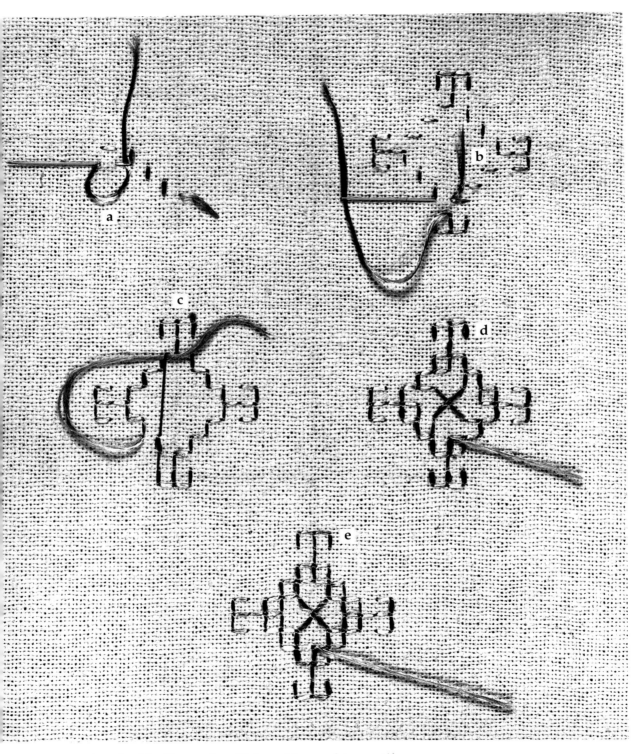

49 *Sample of double running stitch used to complete a motif*

page 53, are exactly the same on both the face and the reverse. A good example of the use of double running stitch is shown in Figure 45.

Originally this work was made as a frieze to decorate a tent, which is why it is long and narrow and embroidered along one side. Today the technique is used, together with other techniques, to decorate fabrics for the home and temple. Figure 49 shows the way in which this work is stitched. The stitching

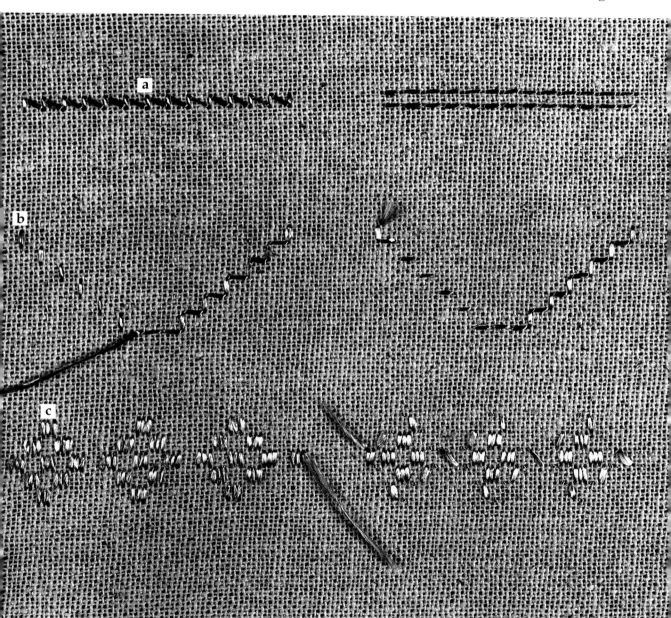

50 *Sample of stitches often used in borders. The face of the stitches is on the left, the reverse on the right*

51 *Detail of a cloth cover, 70 cm (27½ in) square. Gujarat*

52 *Detail of a small cloth, 30 cm (12 in) square. Kutch, Gujarat*

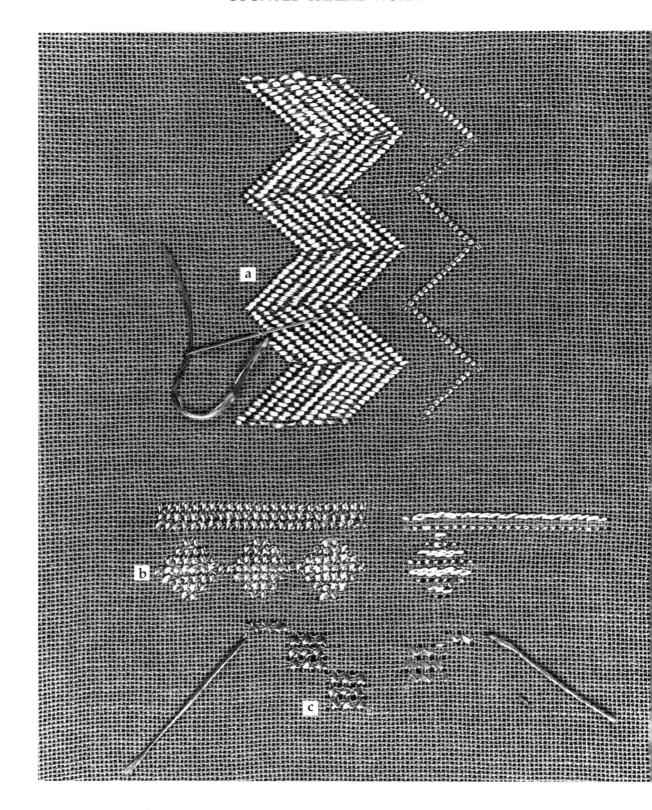

is continuous, the embroiderer following the direction round the motifs and patterns and, at the same time, being aware of the effect on the reverse side. The start of the stitching is shown at (a), with running stitch to complete the first move around the motif to (b). Here one can see the return to the starting point and, when the first part of the outline is completed, any thread ends can be trimmed off. The next stitching round the motif, which completes that section, can be seen at (c). The centre of the motif is then developed as at (d) and completed at (e). A variety of patterns and borders can be created with this double running stitch and variations of it. Some of these can be seen in Figure 50 and include dog-tooth stitch (a), double running steps (b) and running stitch (c), which are used to form block patterns.

There are other examples of counted-thread work which are not included in the general heading of *phulkari*. Figures 51 and 52 show counted-thread work produced in Gujarat. They show cross stitch and florentine stitch used on two different background fabrics. The fabric used in Figure 51 is a jute fabric similar to that used for canvas work. The fabric used in Figure 52 is a close-weave cotton, but the stitching is still very accurate. The stitches used in these two pieces are illustrated in the samples worked in Figure 53. Florentine stitch, shown at (a), is worked in one direction and then another (a small stitch is made under the cloth to change the stitch direction). The reverse (shown on the right) is helpful in illustrating this point. The cross stitch, shown at (b), does not cross the fabric at the back when making a line or a shape. This stitch is made working away from the embroiderer, and it is certainly easier to achieve a rhythm of work if this method is employed. The piece shown in Figure 52 incorporates blocks of cross stitch worked on the diagonal. The method of working this technique can be seen in Figure 53 at (c).

53 (Opposite) Sample of Florentine and cross stitch. The face of the work is on the left, the reverse on the right

4

Whitework

Whitework is stitched on a variety of white or undyed fabrics, from fine to medium weights. On these are worked various combinations of embroidery stitches, including areas of pattern produced by pulled work, eyelets and shadow work with double back stitch and appliqué. Some of these techniques can only be worked on fine, semi-transparent fabrics, and it is for this that Indian whitework is well-known and admired.

The records of travellers in the sixteenth century describe excellent white-work from Bengal, and certainly the work was influenced by the Portuguese traders who founded the port of Hughli at that time, just to the north of Calcutta. The white, counted-thread embroidery produced in the eighteenth century in the Decca, East Bengal (today Dhaka, Bangladesh) was probably taken to Lucknow when Bengali people settled there. By the nineteenth century, Lucknow was producing *chikan* white-work, and this type of whitework was also made in Calcutta and Madras. *Chikan* is the best-known type of Indian

54 Chikan *worker, Lucknow, 1990. The worker is stitching on the wrong side of the fabric, making an area of pulled-thread stitching (see Figure 61[i] on page 74). The surrounding stitches consist of shadow work, as shown in Figure 61[a]). The work is much coarser than the other examples shown in this chapter*

whitework and this, along with other kinds of whitework, were (and still are) produced with a strong foreign as well as

55 *Diagonal stripes and flowers in* chikan *embroidery. Vol VII, no. 257. Sample from the volumes of samples collected by Dr Forbes Watson in the mid-1860s in Deccan, Bengal* (HARRIS MUSEUM AND ART GALLERY, PRESTON)

56 Chikan *muslin embroidery, pulled-thread work. Vol VII, no. 259. Sample from the volumes of samples collected by Dr Forbes Watson in the mid-1860s in Deccan, Bengal* (HARRIS MUSEUM AND ART GALLERY, PRESTON)

an Indian influence on the designs. Where the embroidery was commercialized it was mainly worked by men. Today the men organize the various processes and, as a rule, the women carry out the embroidery. Traditionally, *chikan* embroidery is worked on a very fine white cotton or muslin fabric. The designs are first block-printed on the cloth, and the embroiderer then uses the printed outline as a pattern and guide (see Figure 13 on page 17). The stitches used for this technique are double back stitch and pulled work, as well as running and back stitch (see Figure 61 on page 74). All the stitches used for this work are regular embroidery stitches, but they are applied in a very formal way. Various sizes of needle are used for the stitching, in particular a wide, bluntish one (as shown in Figure 61 at [i]) for the pulled work. Used with the fine cotton fabric and a fine cotton thread, this needle makes the holes in the fabric with ease.

This kind of embroidery has been used for all kinds of items, including sari lengths, clothes, household items and handkerchiefs. In Dr Forbes Watson's samples collected in the mid-1860s

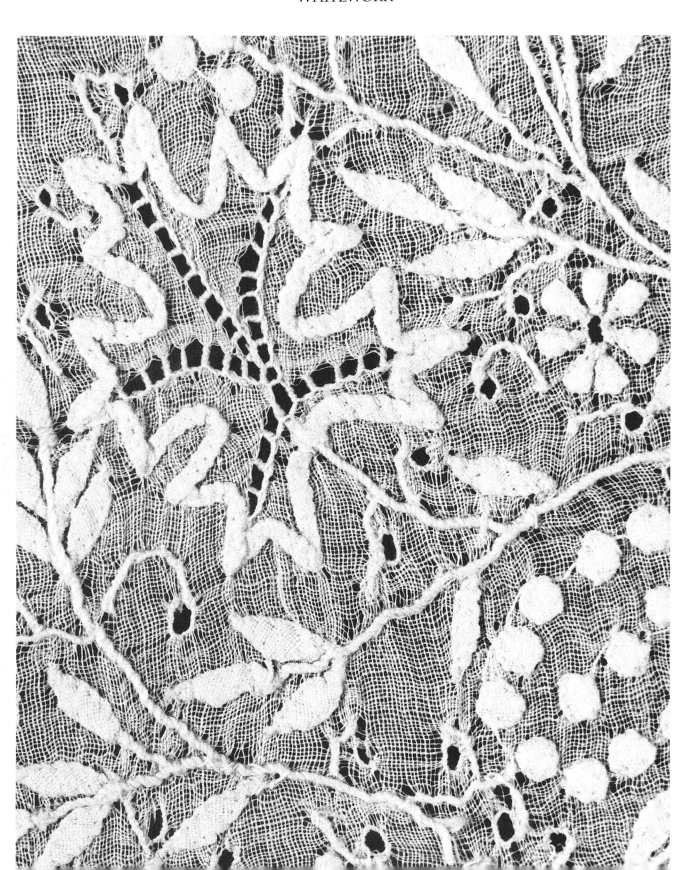

57 (Opposite) The appliqué shown in Figure 60 here forms an outline to a shape and also makes small leaf-like shapes

58 Shadow work, as shown in Figure 61(a). Also eyelets, buttonhole stitch, whipped stem stitch, pulled-thread work, chain stitch and back stitch

59 *Laced running stitch, back stitch, buttonhole and whipped stem stitch*

60 *Sample of* chikan *appliqué. The face of the work is on the left, the reverse on the right*

(see pages 12–13), there are some fine examples of *chikan* embroidery; Figures 55 and 56 show just two from this extensive collection.

Figures 57, 58 and 59 are examples from an archive collection dating from *c*.1850-1930, from an *atelier* for *chikan* embroidery called Kedar Nath Ram, north of Lucknow. The quality of the embroidery is very difficult to appreciate with the naked eye, but these magnified, close-up photographs show the fine stitching and appliqué used.

The *chikan* embroidery produced up to about ten years ago was still of a very high standard, but today it is mainly made quickly and on a larger scale. The quality has consequently diminished, as the exact discipline of working is no longer attended to, the aim being to create the desired effect as speedily as possible. When required to do so, however, the best embroiderers can still produce quality stitching. Much of the stitching is done by women in their spare time. The work is delivered to and collected from their homes, and the block-printing and making-up is carried out elsewhere by other workers.

The techniques of *chikan* embroidery are demonstrated in Figures 60 and 61. Figure 60 shows a type of appliqué at (a). Here a shape is turned under and slip-stitched on to the background fabric. Another appliqué effect is shown at (b), where a strip of fabric is folded so that there is no raw edge, and also folded to produce a curved shape. This shape is placed on the face of the background cloth and is slip-stitched into place.

Figure 61 shows shadow work at (a), and here herringbone stitches are worked close together, with the reverse side of the fabric facing the embroiderer. Double back stitch then appears on the face side of the cloth. As a semi-transparent fabric is used, an opaque shadow is produced. Other forms of stitches worked on this sample are: running stitch (b), laced running stitch (c), couching (d), looped stem stitch (e) and stem stitch (f). Two stages in the formation of an eyelet are shown at (g), and two stages of buttonhole stitch at (h). One of the pulled-thread stitches used in *chikan* work is shown in the form of a zigzag at (i). The stitch is worked with the reverse side facing the embroiderer.

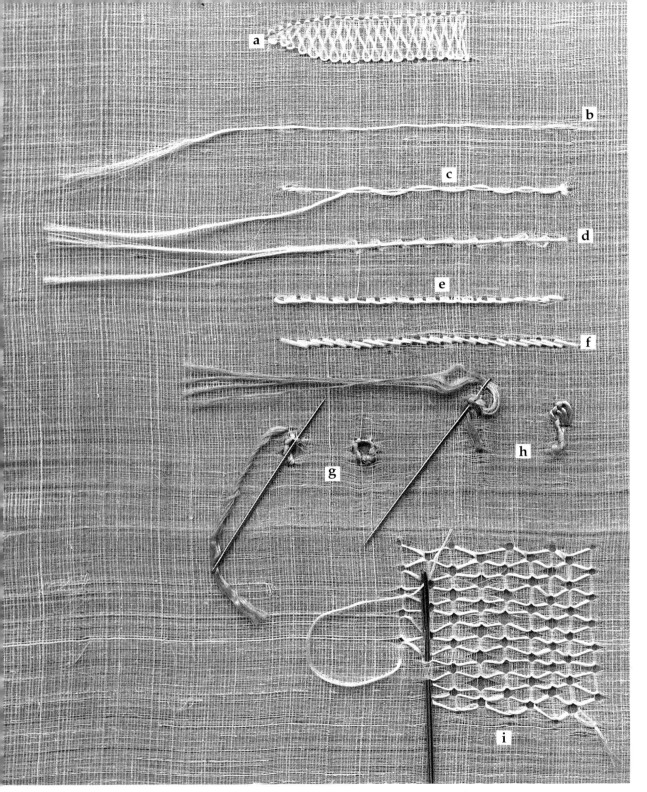

61 *Sample of stitches used in* chikan *embroidery. (a) – (h) show the face of the stitches; the sample at (i) shows the stitch worked on the reverse of the fabric*

5

Mirror work

This embroidery technique is particular to India. Mirror work, also called *shisha* (glass) work, is thought to have been developed by the wife of Shah Jahan, who built the Taj Mahal at Agra in her honour. The technique gained popularity in the seventeenth century. It may have come to India from Baluchistan (now part of Pakistan), or it may have originated in the Gujarat and spread to Rajasthan and the Deccan.

During the Moghal Empire, a process was developed for making glass from sand, lime and soda in a small furnace. From this, glass mirrors were produced for all kinds of uses, one of these being in embroidery. Today, blown glass is silvered and the spheres broken into a few curved pieces, and these in turn are cut with a small, pointed implement into long, thin, oblong pieces. The pieces are then cut into squares and triangles by hand, using the same implement. Scissors are used to make circles and to trim other shapes. The blades of the scissors are loosely hinged so that the inner edges form a 'V' shape.

In the Gujarat, mica may well have been used for decorative purposes before mirrors were developed, as it is found in the grey sands. A late nineteenth-century textile from the Gujarat in the collection at the Calico Museum of Textiles, Ahmedabad (Acc. no. 205), shows a red-silk fabric printed with mica. The piece in Figure 62, which comes from the same period and the same area, contains glass mirrors. It is not known when mica was replaced by mirrored glass for embroidery.

In the Gujarat it is mainly the women, living in the Kutch and Saurashtra areas, who use mirrors in their embroideries. Today they are used in many parts of India. Nomads, who still travel through Rajasthan, Gujarat and the Deccan plateau, use mirrors, and the women embroider the fabric densely round these mirrors so that virtually nothing of the background fabric is visible.

The mirrors come in several sizes and shapes – round, square, triangular, large, small and minute – and some of these are shown at the bottom of Figure 63. The

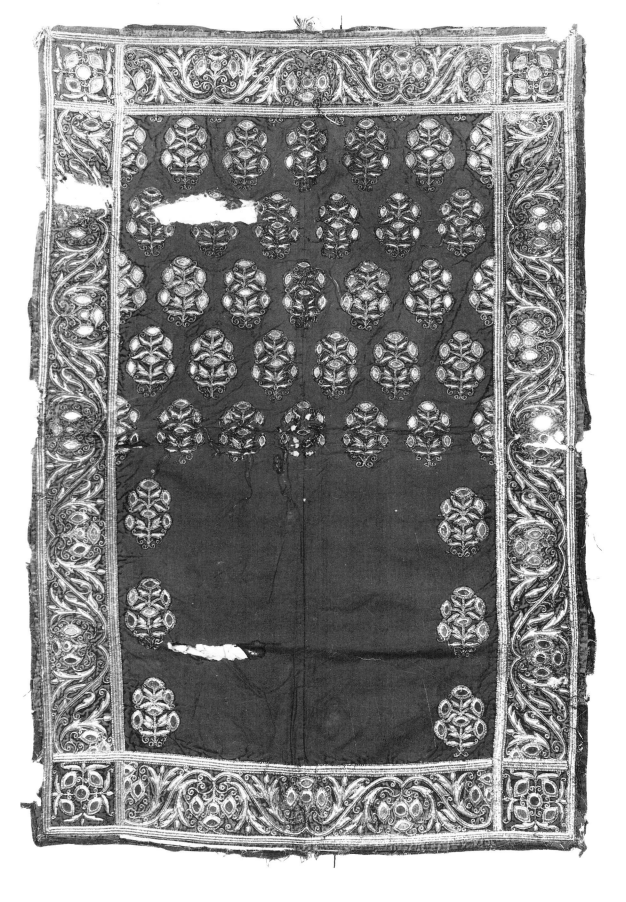

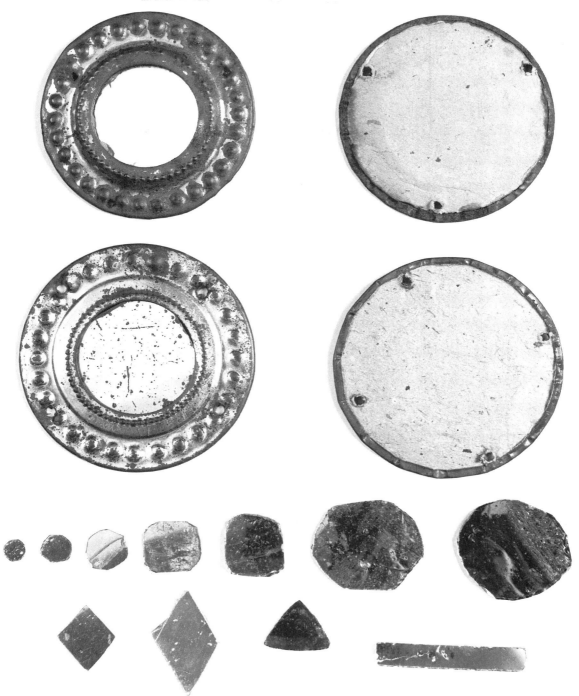

62 (Opposite) Winter Pichhavis (hanging for a Vaishnava temple) velvet zardozi, 133 x 87 cm (52½ x 34 in). The red- and green-velvet ground is embroidered with mirrors and a pure silver wire coated with real gold. Gujarat, late nineteenth century
(ACC. NO. 2161. THE CALICO MUSEUM OF TEXTILES, AHMEDABAD)

63 Mirrors of several sizes and shapes. The fronts of the tin-framed mirrors are on the left, the backs on the right

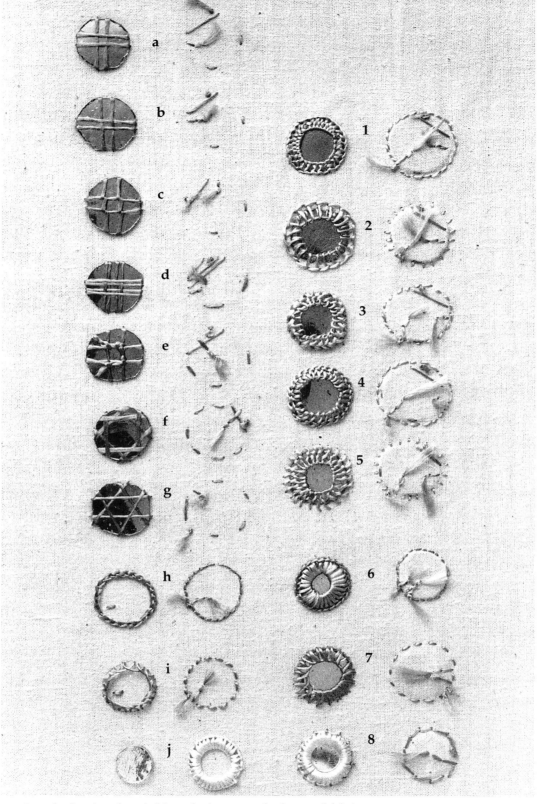

64 *Sample showing the stitching of mirrors to a background fabric*

mirrors have no holes with which to sew them down, so they must be held by the surrounding threads, usually with a form of herringbone stitch.

Round mirrors are the most commonly used and some of these are shown in Figure 64, which also illustrates the stitch formation. The mirror is normally first held in place with two vertical and two horizontal threads, fairly close together; these base threads can be developed as a decorative form in themselves. All the bases used are shown in Figure 64(a)–(g), the most common being those at (a), (b) and (c). In those shown at (d)–(g) there is an additional set of stitches which makes for a stronger base.

The tension of the base stitches is important, as they get pulled out towards the edges of the mirrors by the top stitching: too loose and the mirror falls out; too tight and the stitching is very difficult to pull out from the centre to create a circle of stitches. For convenience, base (b) has been used in the adjoining examples, numbered 1–5, although, of course, the other bases could be used.

The appearance of the stitch can be greatly altered by the tension. A tight tension allows more mirror to be shown and the surrounding stitch to become a fine line; a looser tension makes more of the surround, as can be seen in other photographs in this chapter. The top stitches shown in samples 1–5 are the main ones used. Stitch (1) is known as *shisha*, (2) is buttonhole, (3) is herring-bone, (4) is twisted chain, and (5) is cretan stitch. There are also other methods of forming bases for mirror work. The base used at (h) is a chain stitch, combined with a Ceylon stitch as

65 *Mirrors being put down with a hook. Madras, 1990*

shown at (i), then pulled up to form an enclosure for the mirror, shown at (7).

A method which is becoming increasingly popular uses a ring, covered with thread, which is put on top of a mirror and slip-stitched into place as shown at (j) and (8). This is a quick technique and produces an effect similar to methods traditionally used.

These samples have been worked neatly and formally to illustrate the techniques clearly. When studying actual Indian mirror work, many variations are apparent, and reflect the embroiderer's intention or ability.

Mirrors can also be placed with a hook, as shown in Figure 65. They first have to be held to the fabric with a little adhesive, and are worked over with chain stitch to form a triangular pattern,

68 *Detail of Figure 67(a)*

66 (Opposite) Embroidery to go over a door, embellished with tin-framed mirrors, 107 x 51 cm (42 x 20 in). Gujarat, 1970s

67 Five bands of embroidery using mirror work: (a) belt, Banjara, Central India; (b) belt, southern India; (c) wedding scarf, Kutch, Gujarat; (d) border of a shawl, Kutch, Gujarat; (e) border of a skirt, Kutch, Gujarat

a

b

c

d

e

69 *Detail of Figure 67(b)*

70 *Child's hat. Kutch, Gujarat, 1990*

71 *Child's tunic, green satin, Kutch, Gujarat* (1988.2, GALLERY PURCHASE, MANCHESTER CITY
ART GALLERIES, GALLERY OF ENGLISH COSTUME, PLATT HALL)

72 *Detail of Figure 71*

73 *Child's hood, Kutch, Gujarat* (1988.10, GALLERY PURCHASE, MANCHESTER CITY ART GALLERIES, GALLERY OF ENGLISH COSTUME, PLATT HALL)

74 *Detail of Figure 73*

75 *Small hanging for the home, 54 x 38 cm (21 x 15 in), depicting the god Ganesh. Gujarat, 1980s*

76 *Bag decorated with circular and triangular mirrors, 42 x 31 cm (16½ x 12 in)*

which creates a surround to hold the mirror in place.

Some mirrors have metal surrounds (see Figure 63 on page 77). These tin-framed mirrors have a cardboard backing, and can be stitched on to the fabric through holes in the edge of the tin. The examples in Figure 63 show three holes on the smaller shape and four on the larger one, and they are seen in use in Figure 66, which shows a piece intended to be mounted over a door. Examples of mirror work on clothing can be seen in Figures 5 and 6 (page 13), 19 (page 25) and 70-4 (pages 83–7).

Figure 67 shows some examples of mirror work. The piece at (a) is shown in close-up in Figure 68; the piece at (b) is shown in detail in Figure 69.

Very often mirror work is used with combinations of bright colours (see Figures 70-4). Mirrors are also used in conjunction with a variety of other stitches (see Figures 75 and 76). A detail of Figure 76 is shown in Figure 77, and Figure 78 shows a worked sample of some of the stitches used in this piece. A running stitch worked in a circular manner is seen at (a). The outer circle at (b) is a chain stitch, and the other stitching is buttonhole (c). The circular motif, shown at (d), is all made in chain stitch, with the exception of the central circle which is produced by using both a chain stitch and a buttonhole stitch, as worked at (e).

These stitches are often used without mirrors in the centre, as in Figure 80

77 *Detail of Figure 76*

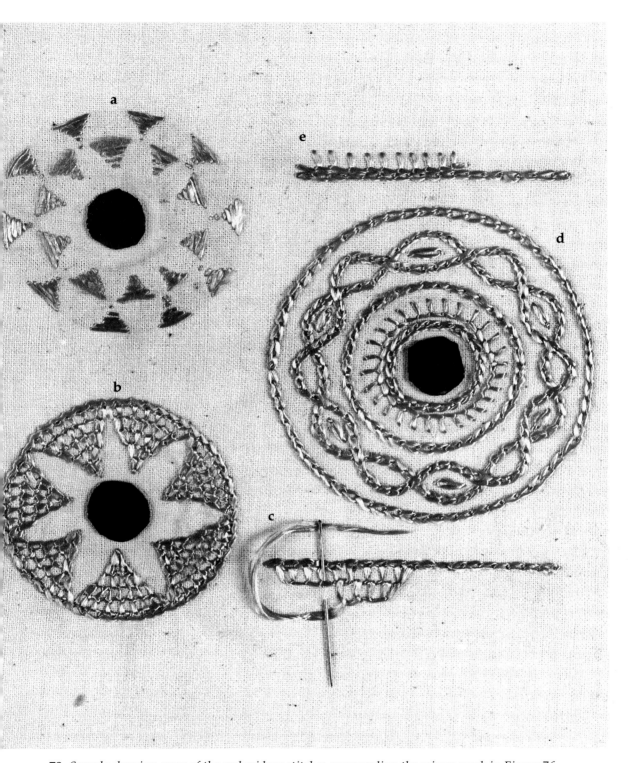

78 *Sample showing some of the embroidery stitches surrounding the mirror work in Figure 76*

(see also the detail in Figure 81). This is an interesting example: it is a 'game' cloth, rather similar to a board game. The centre is a pocket, holding the game pieces when not in use, and the cloth is easily folded or rolled up for transportation.

Figure 82 shows worked examples in which various circles are produced so that the centres are left as a circle of the background fabric. The centres are sometimes filled with an embroidery stitch – usually a herringbone stitch, as shown at (e). The stitch at (a) is simply known as *shisha*. The sample at (b) is formed with a centre in stem stitch; the outer part is a half-herringbone. Through the fabric,

and between these, there is a half-cretan stitch, worked through the stem stitch. The centre of sample (c) is a row of satin stitch. The outer part is a half-herringbone through the fabric and, between these, there is a half-cretan stitch, worked through the satin stitch. The sample seen at (d) is a circle produced with a half-cretan and half-herringbone stitch.

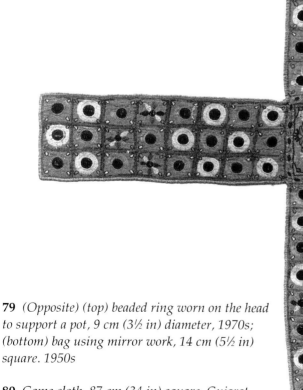

79 *(Opposite) (top) beaded ring worn on the head to support a pot, 9 cm (3½ in) diameter, 1970s; (bottom) bag using mirror work, 14 cm (5½ in) square. 1950s*

80 *Game cloth, 87 cm (34 in) square. Gujarat, mid-twentieth century*

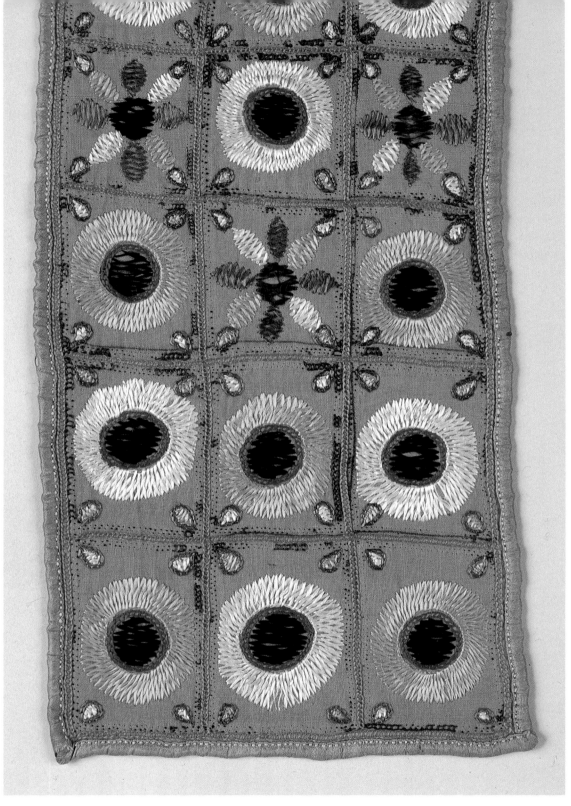

81 *Detail of Figure 80*

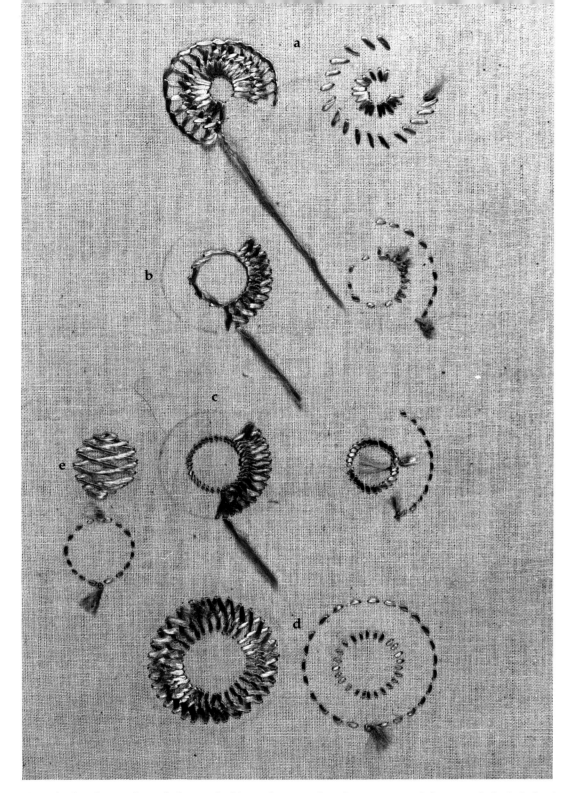

82 *Sample showing various circles worked in such a way that the centres are left as unstitched circles in the background fabric*

6

Metal work

Gold, silver and other metals have been used to enrich embroideries in all parts of India for many years, and these are, perhaps, some of the oldest of all embroidery materials to have been used. In the tenth century, for instance, gold and silver embroidered slippers were exported to Babylon. Some of the processes are thought to have been introduced by the Portuguese. Fabrics which have been embellished by this method include velvet, satin, delicate silk, cotton and muslin, and metal work has been used to enrich trappings, umbrellas, hangings, floor pieces, clothing and other small articles.

In the past, the gold and silver threads used were drawn gold and silver or a mixture of the two (see Figure 62 on page 76), or metal foil wrapped over a core of silk (today this is more likely to be a cotton core). Originally the gold and silver wires and spangles would be just that; today they are imitated in other metals. Metallic ribbons are often used, giving broader lines and a sympathetic finish to edges.

Gold was considered the most sacred metal, symbolizing the sun. Silver was often used as a substitute for gold, and symbolized the moon. Of course, these materials also had an investment and status role to play, as well as adding glitter. Many old examples have now been lost, as owners sell their textiles to recover their investments (the woven and embroidered background can be heated and the precious metals extracted).

Depending on its size, the work is carried out by one or more embroiderers on small or large frames. Workshops in Delhi still produce metal embroidery for items such as saris and bags. Figure 83 shows a piece worked for an umbrella. Many of the designs used today have been in dealers' families for generations; the older designs are perforated on copper foil. The people of other parts of India used gold and silver work together with beads, sequins and embroidered stitches. The workshop in Madras, shown in Figure 84, is typical of such establishments in India today. The seats, trestles and frames have not changed much over the years, as the illustration of an embroiderer in Murshidabad (1785-90) shows (Figure 85).

Gold and silver embroidery was traditionally used for garments in religious ceremonies, and for trappings for elephants, horses and bullocks. To some extent this is still the case today. The most luxurious and best-crafted work was carried out during the reign of the Moghals, when garments, floor-spreads and cushions were produced for the courts. A close examination of embroideries created with this technique reveals a wonderful variety of methods and small differences in applying the wires. The examples in this chapter illustrate some of these techniques. The unfinished piece in Figure 86 shows how gold threads are worked over a base of soft cotton threads (probably weaving thrums). The base threads are stitched through the fabric to fill a shape, and these threads are then stitched over with a length of purl which has been threaded through with a double thread of sewing cotton. The stitching is worked either over and round the shape or up and over the shape (see Figure 92 on page 104). The purls are cut to the required length before they are stitched down.

Gold and silver threads are couched down with a sewing thread. These can be used in a single or double line, or several threads can be couched down together. The lines sometimes pass over each other in order to form the required shapes (see Figure 87). Other variations occur in this work, as can be seen in Figure 92 at (h) and (j), where a sequin is slipped under the couched thread, the couched stitch

83 *Detail of an umbrella, embroidered with purls and sequins. Delhi, 1980s*
(COLLECTION JOHN GILLOW)

being made in the hole of the sequin. All sorts of colours, metals and shapes can be made into a sequin, as seen in Figure 88. Some of these techniques, and others in Figure 89, are shown on the sleeve edge in Figure 87, which illustrates some of the intricate movements which may be achieved when couching with a single line.

84 *Metal-embroidery workshop. Madras, 1990*

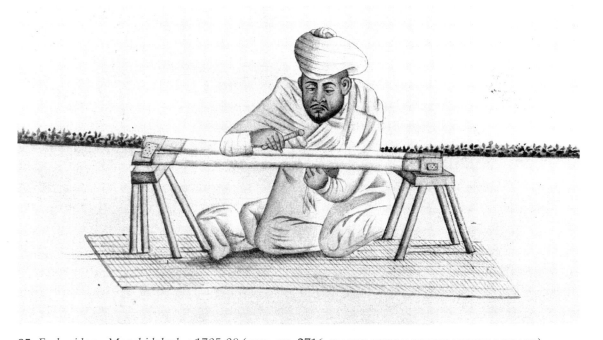

85 *Embroidery, Murshidabad, c.1785-90* (ADD. OR. 2716. BY PERMISSION OF THE BRITISH LIBRARY)

86 *Unfinished peacock motif, 9 x 10 cm (3½ x 4 in). Madras, 1984*

87 *Gold-thread couching and sequins. Cuff of a blouse sleeve. Rajasthan, 1980s*

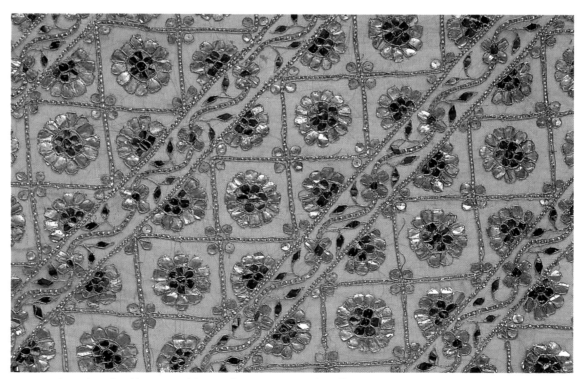

88 *Metal-work embroidery, couching and sequins. Sample collected by Dr Forbes Watson in the mid-1860s, Madras* (HARRIS MUSEUM AND ART GALLERY, PRESTON)

89 *Detail of embroidered muslin gold work. Sample collected by Dr Forbes Watson in the mid-1860s, Madras*
(HARRIS MUSEUM AND ART GALLERY, PRESTON)

Purls are used on their own in several ways: small lines can be created which twist round each other; a longer line can be put down with couching; small pieces of purl can be made to stand up off the surface of the fabric in an arch; or the arch can be held down with another small piece of purl to create a chain-stitch effect, as shown in Figure 92 at (j) and (k).

Purls are sometimes used with sequins, which can be slipped on to the purl if the hole in the sequin is large enough. When sequins with small holes are used, only the fine sewing thread in the centre of the purl goes through the sequin. These purl techniques are used in metal work today (see Figure 83).

Flat lengths of silver or gold plate are also couched down, sometimes over a shape made from card or parchment to give a crisp edge to the shape. Figure 92(i) shows this technique, and it is seen in use in Figures 89, 90 and 91. There are also examples of the metal being used as a thread through the fabric, in which the end of the metal is used instead of a needle.

All the techniques described are best worked on a frame, as the fabric must be kept taut, and both hands need to be free to embroider.

90 *Embroidered muslin, with gold leaf. Sample collected by Dr Forbes Watson in the mid-1860s, Madras* (HARRIS MUSEUM AND ART GALLERY, PRESTON)

91 *Detail of metal embroidery. Sample collected by Dr Forbes Watson in the mid-1860s, Madras*
(HARRIS MUSEUM AND ART GALLERY, PRESTON)

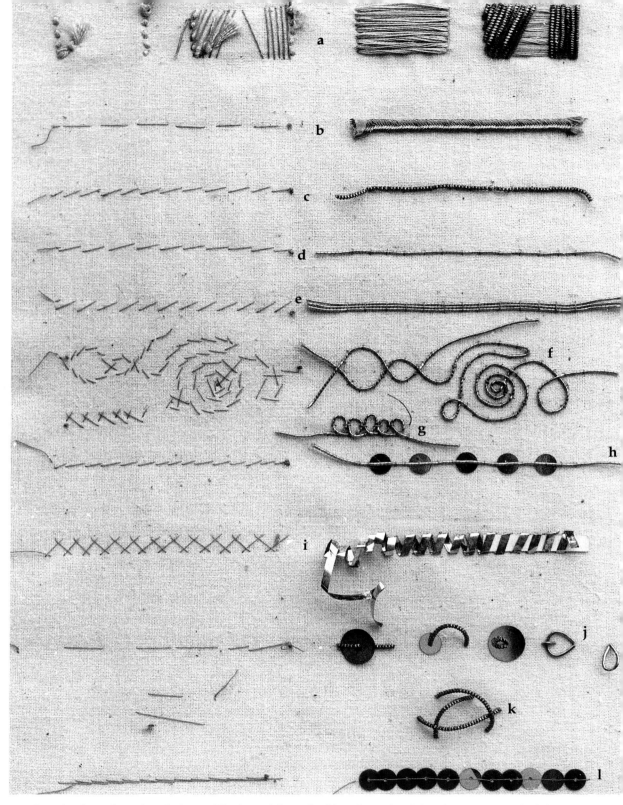

92 *Sample of metal-work techniques. The face of the embroidery is on the right, the reverse on the left*

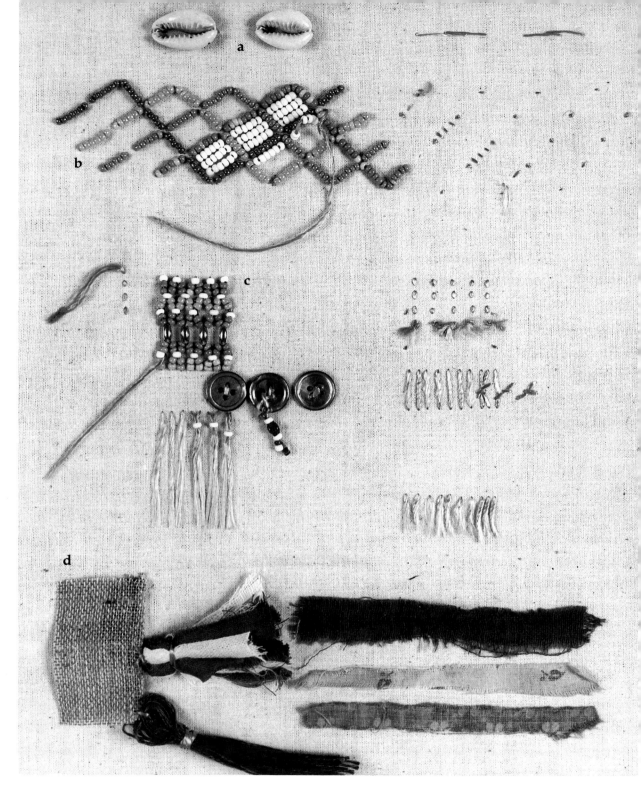

93 *Sample of techniques: (a) cowrie shells; (b) beading, as seen in the beaded ring in Figure 79 on page 92; (c) beading and buttons, detail of a section of Figure 99 on page 110; (d) fabric and thread tassels*

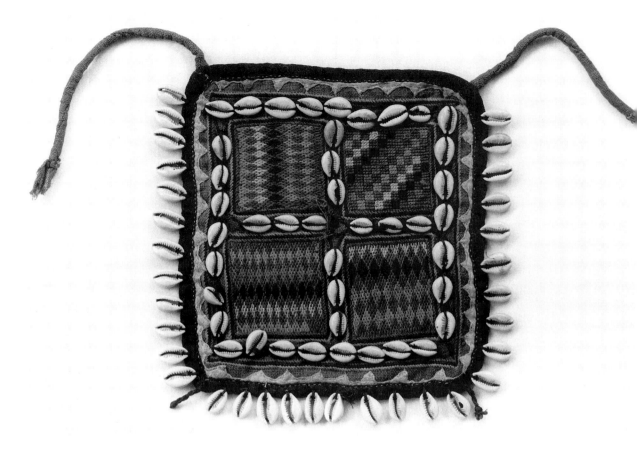

Beads, sequins and other applications

As with mirror work, the tribes wandering through Rajasthan, Gujarat and the Deccan plateau may have spread the use of beads and cowrie shells in embroidery. Cowrie shells are normally sewn on to the main fabric, using the stitch shown in Figure 93(a), although they are sometimes used in the centres and the edges of embroideries, as in Figure 94. Gujarat has been open to external influences from ancient times, and beads of all kinds have been discovered, showing commercial contacts with seafaring people. Beetle wings have been used as a form of sequin to create small shiny areas

94 *Cowrie shells used in the centre and on the edges of the square. Banjara, Deccan*

(see Figure 95 and the detail shown in Figure 96). Sequins have also been made from many other materials, including metals, silver paper and, more recently, plastics. Tassels may be attached to the main part of an embroidery as well as to its edge. Many other objects are applied in addition to tassels and cowrie shells; these include coins and buttons, which are used either on their own, or with beads and threads.

Originally the beads were of European origin. The bead industry in Venice exported them first on other goods, and

95 *Gold and beetle-wing embroidery. Sample collected by Dr Forbes Watson in the mid-1860s, Madras*
(HARRIS MUSEUM AND ART GALLERY, PRESTON)

96 *Detail of Figure 95*

then the beads themselves. By the end of the nineteenth century a particular form of beadwork had developed, centred in the Saurashtra area of Gujarat, and this technique has now been revived. The skill of this work lies in the grading of the size of the beads and the use of colour, as shown in Figures 97 and 98. This particular form of beadwork is perhaps not strictly an embroidery technique, but is really a net-like weave. Figure 93(c) on page 105 shows another example of the bead technique and, in this case, as the beadwork is being made, the threads carrying the beads are stitched through the fabric. A few running stitches are made before the beadwork commences. Beads are often combined with buttons in this way. This sample is similar to the work on the bag shown in Figure 99.

Sometimes whole articles are made by covering cloth forms with beads, such as children's swings, bangles, and the head-rests used for carrying pots (the latter is shown in Figure 79, top, on page 92). The method used is shown in Figure 93 at (b). The needle is brought up through the

cloth, six beads are put on the needle and the thread is caught through the fabric again. This action is then repeated. The number of beads on the needle will depend on whether the main pattern is being formed or whether the infill beads are being put in place.

Fabric tassels are often used on the edges or corners of textiles. They are shown in Figure 93(d) on page 105, made up of strips of various pieces of fabric, folded in half and held together with a thread through the middle of each strip; where they fold over they are held together by binding the thread round the base of the tassel. The tassel is secured to the fabric with two cross stitches loosely stitched to the fabric edge, and ends of thread are 'lost' in the tassel. An unusual feature with thread tassels is that they are sometimes put on edges so that one half of the threads are on one side of the fabric and the other half on the other side. The thread which wrapped the tassel is taken up to the top, and a back stitch through the split top secures it through the fabric.

97 (Above) Embroiderer working on a beadwork door hanging. Rajkot, Gujarat, 1990

98 (Below) Beadwork hanging on a fabric base. Beadwork 19 cm (7½ in) square; outside measurement 39 cm (15½ in) square. Gujarat

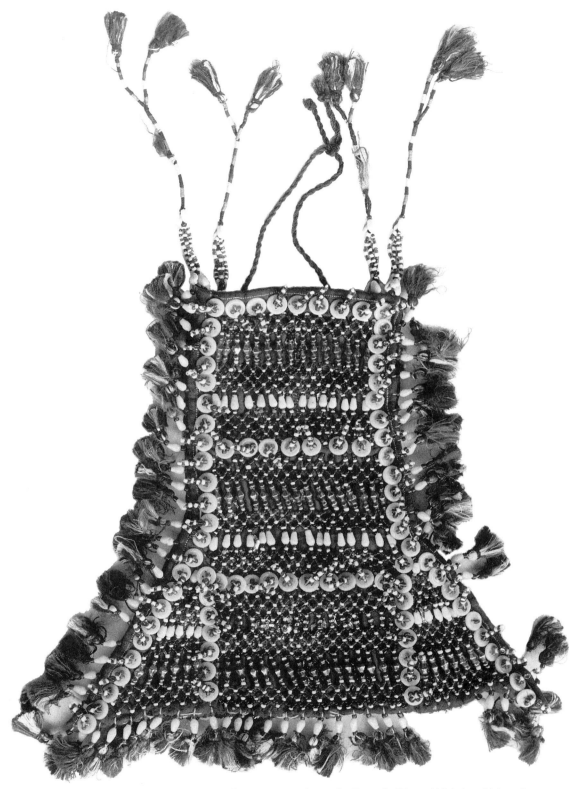

99 *Bag decorated with beads, buttons, silver paper and tassels. Length 25 cm (10 in), width at base 28 cm (11 in). Rajasthan, 1980s*

7

Embroidery
with a hook

There is some uncertainty about the origins of hook embroidery, opinions differing as to whether it originated in China or in India itself. This method of making chain stitch is thought to have been introduced into Kashmir in the sixteenth century, which may support the theory that it was brought from China. However, silk chain-stitch embroideries were exported from the Gujarat at about the same time.

Chain stitch can be produced with a needle or a hook, but greater speed is possible with the latter. The difference between the two methods is particularly noticeable on the back of the work, hook work showing a more regular line, as can be seen in Figure 100 at (f).

In Kashmir, wallhangings, rugs, cushions and furnishing fabrics were traditionally made using this technique, and these are still produced today. In the Kutch, Gujarat, hook work may have developed from the cobbler's awl, used

to decorate the leather of shoes, saddles, bags and other leather goods with embroidery. The same kind of tool is still used today (see Figure 101). The hook is similar, whether embroidering on leather or cloth. It is the handle of the hook that varies; the differing pressures needed when working through a variety of materials means that the hook has to be held differently in the hand, hence the change in the shape of the handle.

This technique can be worked on a frame or in the hand. The method employed really depends on the type of fabric and thread used and on how many embroiderers are working on the same design. Strictly, *ari* is the name of the cobbler's awl, and this is worked in the hand. The tambour is used with a frame (the name comes from the frame), and is worked with a hook set in a pencil-like holder. The hooks can vary according to different work requirements; very fine hooks being used for very fine work, and

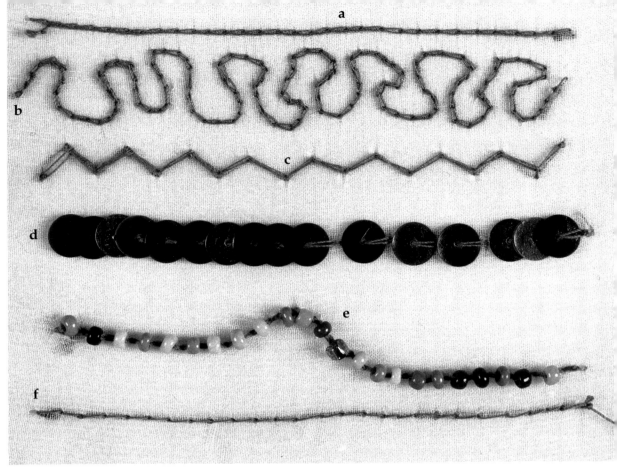

100 (Above) Sample of the main methods: (a) chain stitch; (b) vermicelli; (c) zigzag; (d) sequins, line and spaced; (e) beads; (f) reverse side of a chain stitch

101 (Below) Shoes embroidered with chain stitch, Gujarat, 1990, and embroidered fabric pieces ready to be made into shoes. Rajasthan, 1990

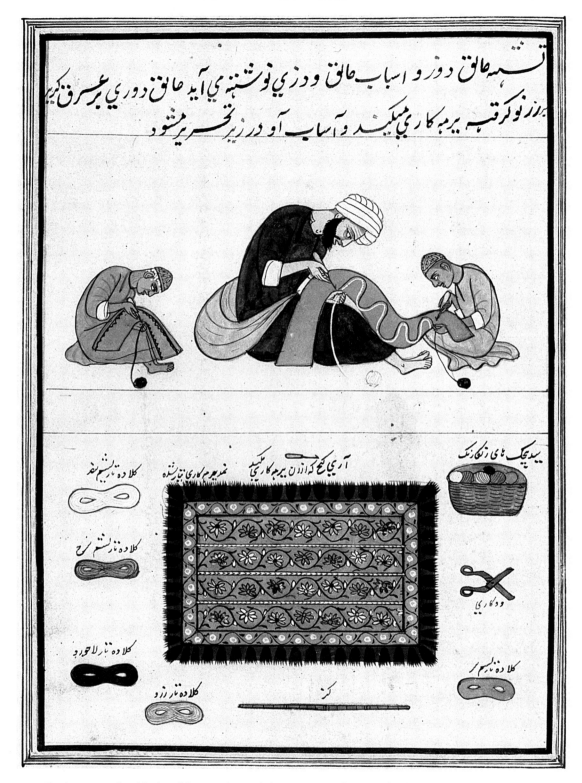

102 *Craftsmen embroidering felt rugs* (namda), *c.1850-60, by a Kashmir artist*
(ADD. OR. 1701, BY PERMISSION OF THE BRITISH LIBRARY)

103 *Rug, 92 x 63 cm (36 x 25 in). Kashmir, 1986*

so on. Hooks have a limited life when used continuously in workshops, and are often made by the embroiderers themselves. Today, hooks are made from a variety of metals, and sources include metal umbrella spokes.

This form of embroidery is done mainly by men in small workshops, and the techniques vary between geographical areas. The base materials used also vary, and the methods used in India are different in some ways from those in Europe. A skilled worker can stitch at speed and bring a certain individuality to the work. Whatever technique is being employed, the embroiderer works with the face of the fabric upwards (the action is to stitch away from oneself whenever possible).

Different types of hook work are produced in Kashmir, Gujarat, and Tamil Nadu. In the Kashmir area, the fabric (which may be woven or felted wool, or cotton) is stitched with an *ari* in wool or silk thread, and today, of course, man-made yarns are used as well. The designs are put on the cloth by the 'prick-and-pounce' method (see page 117). The stitching is worked without a frame and the embroiderers sit cross-legged on the floor with the fabric over their knees. This method has changed little over the years, and rugs similar to that seen in Figure 102 are still made on felted fabric, as shown in Figure 103. The wool thread can also be stitched through a woven cotton fabric (see Figure 104). In these examples two stitches are used – chain and zigzag – and these can be seen worked in Figure 100(b) and (c).

In the Gujarat there were *mochi* embroiderers (the word *mochi* meaning

104 *Section of a length of cloth sold as a furnishing fabric. Kashmir, 1930s*

115

105 *Woman's skirt fragment, 90 x 81 cm (35½ x 32 in). Gujarat, Kutch, nineteenth century. Plain-weave, satin-weave and embroidered* (ACC. NO. 58.2-116, ELIZABETH BAYLEY WILLIS COLLECTION, HENRY ART GALLERY, UNIVERSITY OF WASHINGTON)

shoemaker). These were the professional embroiderers of Kutch. They produced extremely fine hook embroidery without splitting the silk thread. Figure 105 is a fine example of work carried out for the courts by the *mochi*, depicting floral and bird motifs embroidered in chain-stitch hook work (tambour work). The courts have now gone, but this type of embroidery is still produced in the Gujarat, mainly for saris.

This work is done mostly by men, using an *ari*, which is very similar to our tambour hook and, as stated earlier, could well have developed over the years from the cobbler's awl used for leather work. In leather work, the method is to take the hook into the leather, with the hook pointing away from the worker. The thread is looped on to the hook and drawn through the leather back to the face again. A finger guard helps to control the movement and protect the finger, in the same way that a thimble does in regular embroidery. The stitching is produced to embellish all kinds of goods, including shoes, animal trappings and bags.

In Tamil Nadu and Gujarat, the kind of hook work produced by the *mochi*, as seen in Figure 105, continues to be made, but for modern usage. The techniques are similar to those used by European tambour embroiderers. The fabrics are usually semi-transparent and stretched on a frame. The designs are transferred to the fabric by the 'prick-and-pounce' method, using a powder (clay or charcoal) mixed with kerosene. This mixture is put on a cloth pad and pressed through a strong paper (parchment was originally used) on which the design has

106 *Pricked designs on paper (foreground) and a blouse-front design being worked on a frame. Madras, Tamil Nadu, 1990*

been drawn and pricked (see Figure 106). A high proportion of the cost of the work lies in the threads used – gold, silver and silk being used in the better-quality pieces. Cheaper pieces can be produced using cotton, rayon and other metallic threads, the spools of which rest on the floor during stitching. Figure 107 shows a sample of a motif created in metal thread. All workers sit cross-legged on

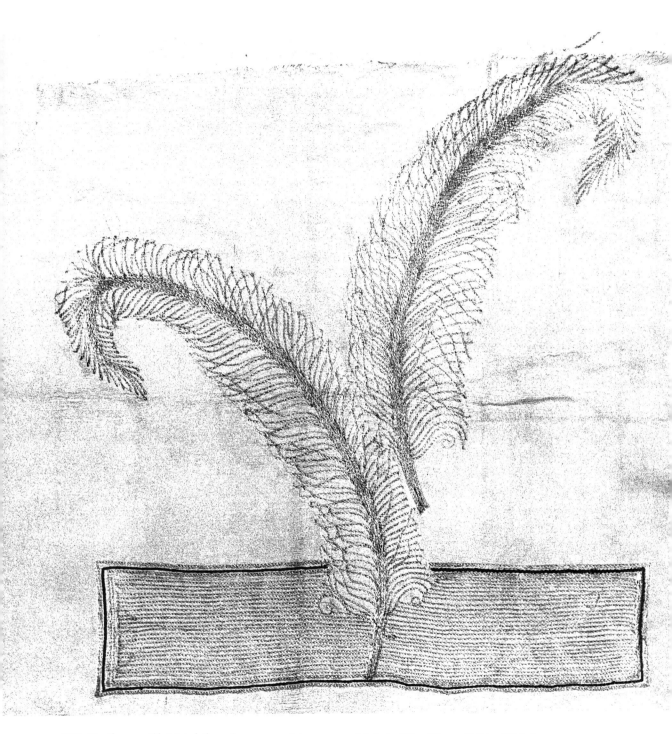

107 *Feather motif. Metal threads on a semi-transparent fabric, 37 x 30 cm (14½ x 12 in). Madras, Tamil Nadu, 1984*

108 *Motif for a sari, 18 x 16 cm (7 x 6 in). Madras, Tamil Nadu, 1984*

the floor and large pieces are worked by several embroiderers sitting on either side of the frame. The hook is put through the fabric, the thread put on the hook, the hook is turned through 90° and pulled up through the fabric to the surface. The hook is then turned back through the 90° (reverse action) to the starting point. The stitching is begun with a knot, a twist in the first chain stitch, or a chain stitch worked back on itself. To finish off, the embroiderer makes a couple of chains on the surface through the lead thread, with an action like that used in crochet. When a line or area of stitches has been completed and another stitched area is to be worked, a long thread is left trailing from one area to the other on the reverse side of the fabric. The next stitch can be worked away from this new point, starting with a chain stitch. This method is employed in the piece in Figure 107. If the next line is to be some distance away, or a new colour is to be introduced to the embroidery, the thread is cut and the new line started in the usual way.

Beads and sequins are applied individually to the front surface of the design from the top, unlike the European method, in which they are on a continuous thread and are worked on the underside. In Indian embroidery, the hook is disconnected from the thread when a bead or sequin is to be attached, as shown in Figure 100 (d) and (e) on page 112. The bead or sequin is pushed high on to the hook, and the hook is then put through the fabric to engage the thread in the usual way. When the hook returns to the surface, the thread is pulled through the bead or sequin before entering the fabric again to make the next stitch. If the next stitch is to have a bead or sequin, the hook is disconnected so that the bead can be placed on the hook. The centre of the piece in Figure 108 shows sequins which have been worked over a grid of chain stitch.

Increasingly, stitches from European tambour work are finding their way into the designs, but the use of chain stitch to hold down mirrors (as in Figure 65 on page 79) is a recent Indian method. This technique really requires a design which can be worked with some continuity and with as few breaks as possible in the stitching, so the route round a motif, flower, border pattern, etc., is important. In this way the speed of embroidering can be maintained, making it a more cost-effective method.

8

Appliqué and patchwork

The main areas in which these techniques are used are Gujarat, Rajasthan, Orissa and Delhi. Appliqué and patchwork fabrics are used for banners, canopies and bags for religious purposes in festivals. They are also used in the home for hangings, long friezes and quilts.

Appliqué is the technique of applying one piece of fabric to another by means of stitchery. Patchwork is sometimes not easy to distinguish from appliqué, both being put on to the ground cloth. However, a patch is normally used to mend a worn fabric or to cover a hole, and this can be done in a decorative way. Patchwork consists of small pieces of cut fabric joined together side by side to make a larger piece of fabric. This technique is found in many parts of the world, and is a delightful way to create decorative fabrics. The Indian examples show some unique approaches. Appliqué and patchwork are methods which are

used extensively and in a wide variety of ways, often in combination with other techniques.

Many fabrics are constructed through cut-and-fold methods, and the shapes produced are then appliquéd to a cloth. Different shapes made by cut-and-fold methods can be used to link other fabric pieces together. Shapes and motifs can be held down with an ordinary sewing thread, or by some type of embroidery stitch that is both functional and decorative.

Some of the patchwork seen in Indian embroideries is combined with many other techniques, and shows remarkable skill and inventiveness in the use of scraps of fabric.

Appliqué

Appliqué shapes are often cut directly from the cloth, the edges turned under and slip-stitched on to the background fabric. If many pieces of one shape are

109 *Door hanging, 79 cm (31 in) square. Gujarat, 1970s*

110 *(Opposite) Sample showing how the centre of Figure 109 is achieved*

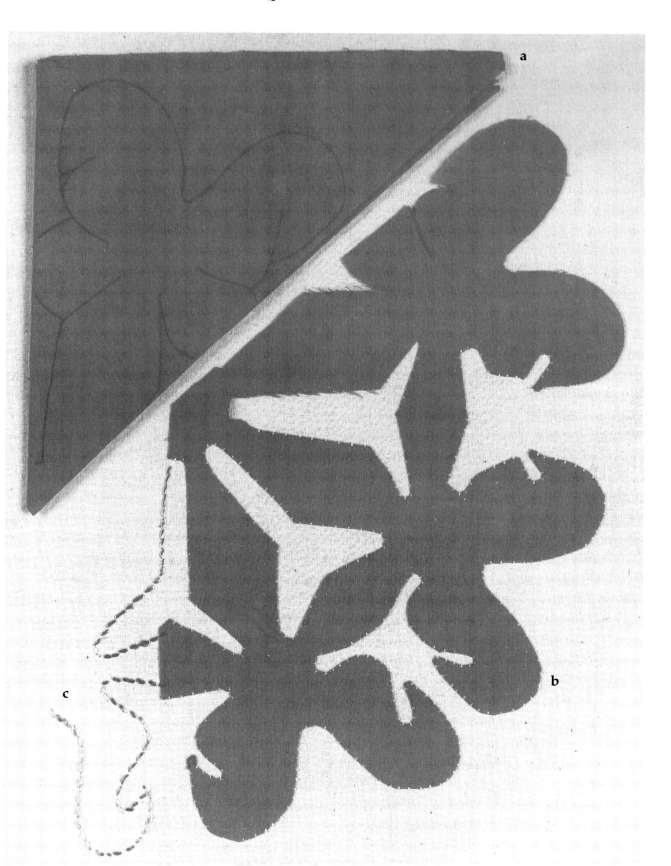

111 *Cover, 60 cm (23½ in) square. Rajasthan, 1980s*

required, a stencil is used. Sometimes embroidery stitches and mirror work are also added. Some of the larger shapes, as shown, for example, in the centre of Figure 109, are made by folding the fabric, cutting pieces out and then opening the fabric out. The edges are turned under and sewn down with a slip-stitch (see Figure 110). This embroidery shows the method of working a piece such as that in the centre of Figure 109. A square of fabric is folded into a triangle, folded again into a smaller triangle and, finally, folded again to achieve the shape seen at (a). The drawn shape on top of this fabric shows the shape to be cut out. When the fabric has been cut it is opened out; this process is a familiar one and is normally used to achieve cut paper shapes.

In (b), a section of appliqué is shown in two stages: the fabric ready to be turned under and slip-stitched, and

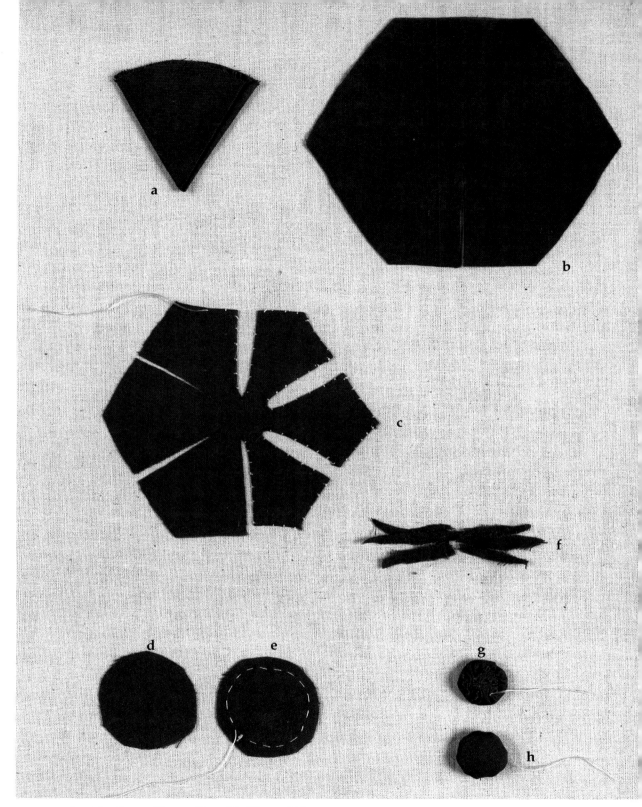

112 *Sample of the flower-like motif used in Figure 111*

when this has been completed. The area shown at (c) is the reverse side of the work (i.e., the reverse of the slip-stitching).

The piece in Figure 111 is a cover from Rajasthan. The centre has been made in the same way as the centre of Figure 109. The interest in this piece lies in the way in which the small, flower-like shapes have been produced, and this is shown in more detail in the sample worked in Figure 112. A roughly cut circle of fabric is folded first in half, and then into three, and cut to make a curved edge at (a). When opened out, the resulting shape is seen at (b). Cuts are made towards the centre of the shape, and the edges turned under as in (c). A centre is made from a circle of fabric (d), with a running stitch round the edge at (e). The shape is then drawn up over a filling of small pieces of fabric, shown at (f). The back of the drawn-up circle is shown at (g), and the front at (h). The shape (h) is placed in the centre of shape (c) and it then appears as if all the petal-like shapes were cut in separate pieces.

The wallhanging in Figure 113 (of which a detail is shown in Figure 114), from Delhi, illustrates the use of embroidery stitches with appliqué. The applied shapes are held down with a slip-stitch and then embroidered. Sometimes the shapes are held down just with embroidery stitches and no sewing is used, as in Figure 115(c). The samples in Figure 115 show some of the techniques employed in the example shown in Figure 113, illustrating how embroidery stitches are used for both practical and decorative purposes. The use of a couched line on the edge of the

applied shape is shown at (a). Definition is added to the shape with herringbone and chain stitch at (b), and with a cross-form stitch at (d). Folded strips of cloth are held down with flat strips of cloth as at (e). In Orissa, embroidery stitches are used with this method. Figure 116 shows decorative embroidery stitches holding down appliqué shapes (the elephants and lotus plant), as well as being used to define the shapes. The main stitches are chain and running stitch.

Fold, cut and press method

In Pipli and Puri in Orissa, it is thought that these techniques have been used to decorate the temple since AD 1054, and perhaps well before that date. They were also produced for the houses of the rulers and the wealthy. It is mainly the men who are involved in making these pieces, and the techniques are handed down from father to son. Increasingly, sewing machines are used, but many pieces can only be created by hand or need only a small stitch to hold something in place. Some of the folding and stitching methods are still exclusive to this part of India.

Some of the processes used in the pieces from Orissa (Figures 117 and 118) are shown on the samples in Figure 119. The work is particular to this area and, although the same techniques are used today, they are not made with the same skill and care. The pieces from Orissa show ruched circles produced by the method shown in Figure 119 at (b). The centres of the circles are not always treated in the same way: sometimes they are left empty and sometimes they are

113 *Wallhanging, 150 cm (69 in) square. Delhi, 1980s*

114 *Detail of Figure 113*

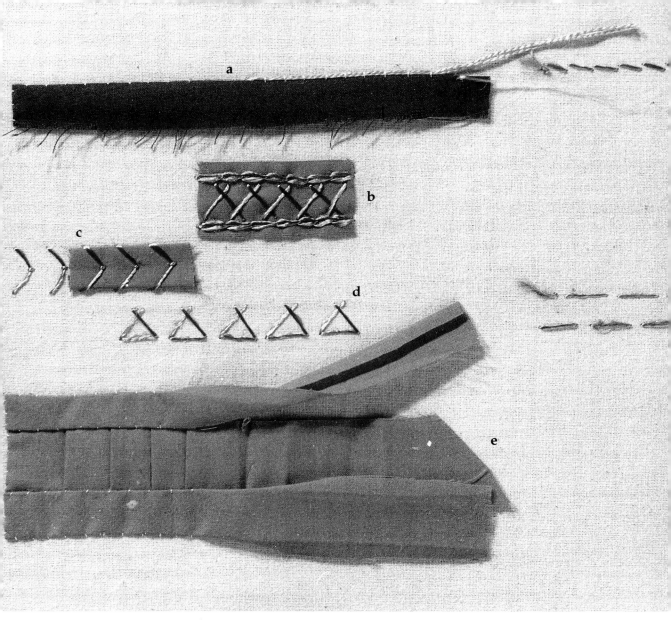

filled with a plain circle of fabric, held
down with a small stitch. The ground of
the piece in Figure 117 is worked with
swirls of chain stitch, and the same stitch
is used on the applied shapes of parrots,
rahu (a demon), the sun, the moon, a
tree and lions, the stitching cleverly
'drawing' into the shapes. The whole is
in the shape of a betel leaf.

The process shown in Figure 119 at (a)
is used to link parts of a hanging together,

115 *Sample of some of the techniques used in
Figure 113. The face of the work is shown on the
left, the reverse of (a) and (d) on the right*

i.e., they are not put on to a background
fabric, but strips of embroidery and
appliqué are linked together. This
method is used in Figure 118. Figure 119
shows a series of worked examples. A
plain piece of fabric is shown at (a1). This

116 *Pipli, Orissa, 1990*

piece is folded over towards the centre at (a2), and at (a3) the folded strip forms a zigzag shape. Another strip of fabric is shown at (b1), and folded in half at (b2). The piece is then stitched with a running stitch (b3), the fabric is drawn up with the running-stitch thread, and the ends are joined with an overcast stitch. The flower motif is seen at (b4), while (b5) shows a circle of fabric drawn up by running stitch round the edge and filled with scraps of fabric. This shape is placed in the centre of the circle. The piece of fabric shown at (c1) is folded and pressed at (c2) and turned over at (c3). The pieces are then placed alongside each other at (c4) with the extending pieces carefully tucked in. A circle is formed with the

eight folded pieces. This whole shape is then sewn down in various ways.

The worked samples in Figure 120 represent another form of folded, cut and pressed work. This shows a method of using triangles in strips which are cut, pressed and used in various ways in embroideries. This method is thought to originate in Orissa.

The original strip of fabric is shown at (a1). This strip is cut through at equal intervals, the cuts not quite extending through the whole strip. The fabric is folded back to produce the triangular shapes at (a3) and the whole is slip-stitched on to the background fabric.

117 *Betel leaf shape, probably from a fan, 97 x 85 cm (38 x 33½ in). Appliqué and embroidery on a velvet background fabric. Puri, Orissa, early twentieth century*

Another approach is shown at (b), where the strip of triangles is sewn to another strip of fabric, between the triangular piece and the background fabric. A further variation can be seen at (c). Here the strip of triangles is positioned near the edge of another fabric, which is turned in and over the base of the triangles (rather like a hem) and held in place with a row of running stitches. A strip of triangles can be set into a seam or join, as shown in (d). In this instance a plain strip has been stitched on one piece of fabric. The two fabrics are prepared first and then sewn together with running stitch.

118 *Detail of a hanging. Folded cloth strips and folded flower shapes. Chain stitch and buttonhole embroidery. Puri, Orissa, late nineteenth century*

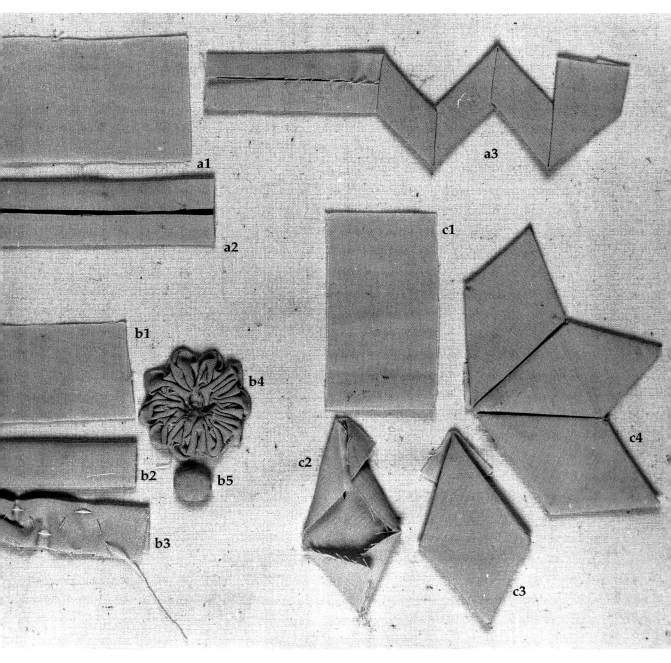

119 *Sample showing fold, cut and press methods*

120 *Sample showing how strips of triangles are made*

121 *Part of a cover, Rajasthan, 1980s* (COLLECTION OF ISABEL WRIGHT)

122 *Sample showing the processes used to achieve the border in Figure 121*

Patchwork

Patchwork is commonly understood to be the process in which fabrics which are (or were) in daily use are joined together in small pieces to form larger, decorative pieces. Often patchwork is used on its own, although sometimes it is used with other processes. It is this multiplicity of combinations of patchwork and related techniques which illustrates the cleverness of Indian embroiderers.

The cover in Figure 121 shows patchwork fabrics linked with piped seams to plain and appliquéd fabrics. The overall effect is to link the fabrics together in an unobtrusive way, the limitation of colours also helping to integrate them.

Figure 122 illustrates the processes of patchwork and joining techniques used to produce the effects seen in the previous piece. Here there is a piece of white fabric (b), on which a blue and a red shape have been placed and slip-stitched down. The two pieces, (a) and (b), are joined together with a folded piece of white fabric (piping). The chevron pieces, shown at (c), are made up of pieces similar to those at (d), which are held together with a row of running stitches, as in (e). These are, in turn, joined to (b) with a strip of white piping between (b) and (c). Another row of patchwork, made from the pieces shown at (f) and (g), makes up the next strip in the piece, which is similarly linked to (c).

These illustrations show some of the unusual appliqué and patchwork processes used by Indian embroiderers. They are very resourceful indeed, recycling old fabrics into lovely new pieces which may be used for a range of decorative household items.

Stitch techniques

123 *BACK STITCH*
This makes a neat, regular line. The reverse of this stitch is a stem stitch

124 *BEADWORK*
One or more beads are taken up by the needle. A single bead is secured by a single stitch

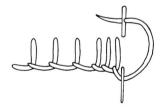

125 *BUTTONHOLE STITCH*
Buttonhole stitch can be worked in lines on fabric or on the edge of fabric (sometimes then referred to as blanket stitch), with various spacings of the stitch. It is also used in little groups of three to make a small spot

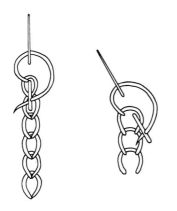

126 *CHAIN STITCH and OPEN CHAIN STITCH*
The line of stitches is worked away from the embroiderer. Lines are made by using both types of stitch

127 *COUCHING*
The laid thread can be metal or cord, and is often a thread that could not be sewn through the fabric

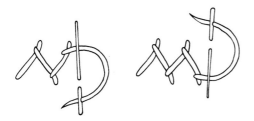

128 *CRETAN STITCH*
This stitch is used in a variety of ways: as a base thread to 'draw' the design out on the fabric; as a stitch forming lines; or for patterns or blocks of stitchery. It is also used in mirror work and other circles of embroidery stitches, often in conjunction with herringbone stitch

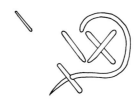

129 *CROSS STITCH*
The cross can be worked on its own, in a row, or to make a variety of patterns. It is often used in counted embroidery. This diagram shows one of the most frequently used methods (the reverse dog-tooth stitch) but a look at the back of embroideries reveals a number of ways of taking the thread from one cross to another

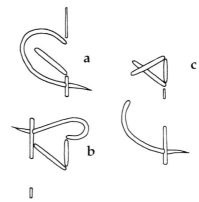

130 *CROSS-FORM STITCH*
This is one of the stitches that is particular to Indian embroidery. It has the interesting feature that, though it is worked towards the embroiderer, the stitches develop in the direction away from the embroiderer

131 *DOG-TOOTH STITCH*
The reverse of this stitch looks like a double row of back stitch

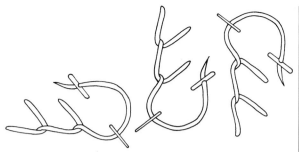

132 FEATHER STITCH

This stitch is similar to buttonhole stitch and open chain stitch. It is worked in any direction, depending on where the stitches are being embroidered

133 FLY STITCH

The stitch holding the 'V' shape in place can be made longer. The stitch can be used singly, or in rows to make patterns. It is also used to hold down strips of fabric and braids

134 HERRINGBONE STITCH

This is a very versatile stitch. The diagram shows it being worked in the usual way, but the stitches only have to be worked closer together, another row worked on top, or the row interlaced, and the effect changes. If the stitches are worked close together (close herringbone stitch), the small amount of thread on the reverse of the fabric will appear as a double back stitch.

When close herringbone stitch is worked on a semi-transparent fabric, the reverse is used as the face of the embroidery, and the result is called shadow work

135 INTERLACING

In this diagram, the interlacing has been worked over a base of herringbone stitch, although other base stitches are used in some instances. The base has to be regular, so that the motif or pattern can be interlaced in a regular and symmetrical way

 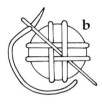 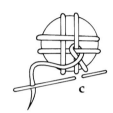

a   **b**   **c**

136 MIRROR WORK

(a) the base stitch (see Figure 64[b] on page 78)
(b) the first top stitch (Figure 64[3])
(c) the top stitch used to pull the base threads out to form a neat centre

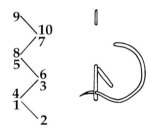

137 PULLED-THREAD CHIKAN

These stitches are formed with a wide blunt needle. They are tightly tensioned so that the fabric becomes distorted, and the holes formed are created at the points where the needle enters and leaves the fabric

138 PURL

A piece of purl has been cut and threaded through the needle

139 *ROMANIAN STITCH, also known as*
INDIAN FILLING STITCH
This is used in a variety of ways: radiating
round a circle, the stitches separately
creating a little mark, or as a close filling
stitch

141 *STEM STITCH*
The angle of the line formed by this stitch
can vary and, when used horizontally, it is
the reverse of a back stitch

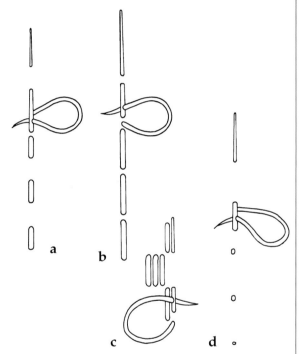

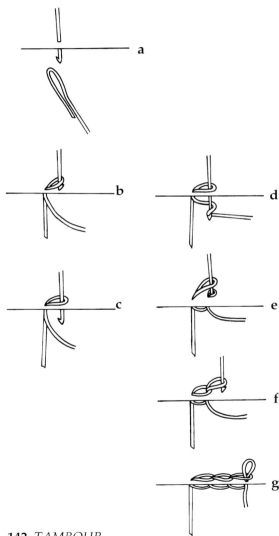

140 *RUNNING or DARNING STITCH*
A simple stitch which can achieve very
effective results. (a) and (b) show how the
space between each stitch can be varied.
Lines can be put together with the same
spacing or varied spacing, and in this way,
various darning patterns are produced.
(c) Running stitch can be used to produce
blocks of stitches in a reversible pattern.
(d) A small stitch is made, working with the
reverse of the fabric facing the embroiderer.
It is easier to make an accurate counted
pattern with this method

142 *TAMBOUR*
These diagrams show the sequence of
movements used to create a series of chain
stitches by the tambour method

Further reading

Books

BHAVNANI, ENAKSHI, *Folk and Tribal Designs of India*, Taraporevala, 1974

BROADBENT, MOIRA, *Animal Regalia*, Portia Press, 1985

BUTLER, ANNE, *The Batsford Encyclopedia of Embroidery Stitches*, Batsford, 1983

CHATTOPADHYAY, KAMALADEVI, *Indian Embroidery*, Wiley Eastern, 1977

COLLINGWOOD, PETER, *Textile and Weaving Structures*, Batsford, 1987, pp 154-9

CRILL, ROSEMARY, *Hats from India*, Victoria and Albert Museum, 1985

DHAMIJA, JASLEEN (ed), 'Living Traditions in India', *Crafts of the Gujarat*, Mapin International, New York, 1985

DONGERKERY, KAMALA S., *Romance of Indian Embroidery*, Bombay, 1954

DONGERKERY, KAMALA S., *The Indian Sari*, The All-Indian Handicrafts Board, New Delhi, nd

DUBIN, LOIS SHERR, *The History of Beads*, Thames and Hudson, 1987, pp 181-200

DURRANS, B. and KNOX, R., *India: Past into Present*, British Museum, 1982

ELSON, V.C., *Dowries from Kutch: A Women's Folk Tradition in India*, University of California, 1979

EMERY, IRENE, *The Primary Structures of Fabric*, Arno, New York, 1972

GILL, HARJEET SINGH, *A Phulkari from Bhatinda*, Punjabi University, Patiala, 1977

GROSS, NANCY D. and FONTANA, FRANK, *Shisha Embroidery*, Dover Publications, 1981

Indian Embroidery, Victoria and Albert Museum, 1951

IRWIN, JOHN and HALL, MARGARET, *Indian Embroideries*, vol II, Ahmedabad, 1973

IWATATE, HIROKO, *Desert Village, Life and Crafts, Gujarat, Rajasthan*, Yobisha, 1989

JOHNSON, B., *Advanced Embroidery Techniques*, Batsford, 1983, pp 123-56

MEHTA, RUSTAM J., *Masterpieces of Indian Textiles*, Bombay, 1979

MOHANTY, BIJOY CHANDRA, *Appliqué Craft of Orissa*, The Calico Museum of Textiles, Ahmedabad, 1980

NABHOLZ-KARTASCHOFF, MARIE-LOUISE, *Golden Sprays and Scarlet Flowers*, Shikosha, Japan, 1986

NICHOLSON, JULIA, *Traditional Indian Arts of Gujarat*, Leicester Museums, publication no. 95, 1988

ORCHARD, WILLIAM C., *Beads and Beadwork of American Indians*, Museum of the American Indian, Heye Foundation, 1975, pp 104-50

ROBINSON, FRANCIS (ed), *The Cambridge Encyclopedia of India, Pakistan, Bangladesh, Sri Lanka*, Cambridge University Press, 1989

WATT, SIR GEORGE, *Indian Art at Delhi 1903*, John Murray, 1904

WELCH, S.C., *Indian Art and Culture*, Metropolitan Museum, New York, 1985

WHEELER, MONROE (ed), *Textiles and Ornaments of India*, Arno, New York, 1972

YACOPINO, FELICCIA, *Threadlines Pakistan*, Ministry of Industries, Government of Pakistan, 1977

ZAMAN, NIAZ, *The Art of Kantha Embroidery*, Bangladesh Shilpakala Academy, 1981

Magazine articles

BANERJI, ADRIS, 'Phulkaris: A Folk Art of the Punjab', *Marg*, June 1955, vol VIII, no. 2, pp 59-64

BÉRINSTAIN, VALÉRIÉ, 'An Early Jain Embroidery', *Marg*, vol XL, no. 3, pp 2-3

BÉRINSTAIN, VALÉRIÉ, 'Early Indian Textiles discovered in Egypt', *Marg*, vol. XL, no. 3, pp 16-24

DHAMIJA, JASLEEN, 'Kashida, Sujani and Appliqué', *Marg*, December 1966, vol XX, part 1

KRAMRISCH, STELLA, 'Kanthas of Bengal', *Marg*, June 1955, vol VIII, no. 2, pp 59-64

'Bihar Handicrafts', *Marg*, December 1966, vol XX, no. 1

'Embroidery Issue', *Marg*, March 1964, vol VIII, no. 2

'Embroidery (Rajastani Handicrafts)', *Marg*, December 1964, vol XVIII, no. 1, pp 20-31

BROADBENT, MOIRA, 'Animal Regalia from North West India and Pakistan', *Embroidery*, 1985, vol 36, no. 4, pp 128-9

CASSIDY, ROSEMARY, 'Kashmiri Embroidery', *Embroidery*, 1986, vol 37, no. 3, pp 100-1

HAMER, LOUISE, 'Indian Textiles from the Embroiderers' Guild Collection', *Embroidery*, 1986, vol 37, no. 4, p 156

HARRIS, KATHLEEN, 'Indian Embroidery', *The Embroideress*, 1934, vol VII, p 36

HOWELL-SMITH, A.D., 'Indian Embroidery', *Embroidery*, 1935, vol 11, p 3

IRWIN, JOHN, 'Indo-European Embroidery', *Embroidery*, 1959, vol X, p 1

RAFFE, W.G., 'Embroideries of India', *The Embroideress*, 1937-9, vols X-XIII

BÉRINSTAIN, VALÉRIÉ, 'Mughal Style', *Hali*, 1990, no. 54, pp 116-21

COHEN, STEVEN, 'Hanging Gardens', *Hali*, 1985, no. 28, pp 41-5

CRILL, ROSEMARY, 'Topis and Turbans', *Hali*, 1985, no. 28, pp 46-7

Other useful publications

CLARK, STANLEY, 'Indo-Dutch Embroideries of the Seventeenth Century', *Needle and Thread*, no. 11, April 1914, pp 29-31

FRATER, JUDY, 'The Meaning of Folk Art in Rabari Life', *Textile Museum Journal*, 1975, vol IV, no. 2, pp 47-60

IRWIN, JOHN, 'The Commercial Embroidery of Gujarat in the Seventeenth Century', *Journal of the Indian Society of Oriental Art*, vol XVII, 1949

IRWIN, JOHN, 'Indo-Portuguese Embroideries of Bengal', *Journal of Royal India, Pakistan and Ceylon Society*, vol XXVI, part 2, 1951

JAYAKAR, PUPUL, 'Embroidery of Gujarat', *Times of India Annual*, 1966

KRAMRISCH, STELLA, 'Kantha', *Journal of the Indian Society of Oriental Art*, vol VII, 1939, pp 141-67

RSA Journal, vol CXXXVI, no. 5378, January 1988, pp 116-31

SINGH, PURAN, 'Some Rumals from Chamba', *Rupam*, vol XXXII, 1927

STEEL, MRS F.A., 'Phulkari Work in the Punjab', *Journal of Indian Art*, vol II, 1988

'Stitches and Methods of Work - 1', *Needle and Thread*, no. 1, January 1914, pp 11-15

List of suppliers

Rayon embroidery floss
Endmar Co.
P.O. Box 55
Camarillo, CA 93011
(805) 484-2306

Metallic and silk floss
Kreinik
9199 Riesterstown Rd. Ste. 209B
Owings Mills, MD 21117
(800) 537-2166

Tambour hooks
Lacis
3163 Adeline Street
Berkeley, CA 94703
(510) 843-7178

Mirrors and other embroidery items
Evening Star Designs
69 Coolidge Ave. #P
Haverhill, MA 01832
(800) 666-3562

Publications
Art Book Center
Madalpur
Ellis Bridge
Almedabad — 380 006
India

Calico Museum of Textiles
Sarabhai Foundation
The Retreat
Shahibag
Ahmedabad 380 004
India

Marg Publications
Army and Navy Building (3rd floor)
148 Mahatma Gandhi Road
Bombay — 4000 023
India

Collections

A.E.D.T.A. (Association pour l'Etude et la Documentation des Textiles d'Asie), 60 Bis, Avenue de Breteuil, 75007 Paris, France

The Calico Museum of Textiles, Sarabhai Foundation, The Retreat, Shahibag, Ahmedabad 380 004, India

Victoria and Albert Museum, South Kensington, London SW7 2RL, England

For details of other museum collections, refer to Cecil Lubell (ed), *Textile Collections of the World:* vol 1 *United States and Canada,* 1976; vol 2 *United Kingdom and Ireland,* 1976; vol 3 *France,* 1978, Studio Vista

Index